Tutor

Ruth Johnson Colvin

A COLLABORATIVE, LEARNER-CENTERED APPROACH TO LITERACY INSTRUCTION FOR TEENS AND ADULTS

New Readers Press
ProLiteracy's publishing division

TUTOR, 8th Edition
ISBN 978-1-56420-895-8

Copyright © 2009 New Readers Press; 1993, 1987, 1984, 1981, 1976, 1974 by
Literacy Volunteers of America, Inc.; 1972 by Follett Publishing Co.
New Readers Press
ProLiteracy's Publishing Division
104 Marcellus Street, Syracuse, New York 13204
www.newreaderspress.com

Printed in the United States of America
9 8 7 6 5 4

Proceeds from the sale of New Readers Press materials support professional
development, training, and technical assistance programs of ProLiteracy
that benefit local literacy programs in the U.S. and around the globe.

Contributing Authors: Corinne Smith, Ph.D. (chapter 10); Jane Root, Ph.D (*Tutor* 1–6);
Judy Cheatham, Ph.D (*Tutor* 7); Lester Laminack, Ed.D (*Tutor* 7)
Editor: Beth Oddy
Designer: Andrea Woodbury
Art and Design Supervisor: James Wallace
Production Specialist: Maryellen Casey
Cover Design: Carolyn Wallace

ABOUT THE AUTHOR

For years, literacy as a global mission interested Ruth Johnson Colvin. When she learned that there were over 11,000 people functioning at the lowest level of literacy in her own city of Syracuse, NY, she decided to do something about it. So in 1962, she started Literacy Volunteers of America, Inc. (LVA), one of the organizations that merged to form ProLiteracy. LVA trained volunteers to teach adult basic literacy and English to speakers of other languages, one-on-one or in small groups. Mrs. Colvin stresses the importance of a learner-centered, collaborative approach to teaching.

The recipient of nine honorary doctorates, Mrs. Colvin also was given the highest award for volunteers in the United States—the President's Volunteer Action Award, presented by then President Ronald Reagan in 1987. In 2006, she received the Presidential Medal of Freedom, the highest award given to a civilian, presented by then President George W. Bush. She was inducted in the National Women's Hall of Fame in 1991.

Mrs. Colvin has traveled across the United States and around the world, visiting 62 countries and giving training in 26 developing countries. In a richly varied and exemplary career, she has found most meaningful the experiences where she assisted and encouraged practical, grass root ventures. Mrs. Colvin continues to work with top professionals in the field, putting the latest research into layman's language and providing how-to teaching techniques.

ABOUT PROLITERACY

ProLiteracy champions the power of literacy to improve the lives of adults and their families, communities, and societies. We envision a world in which everyone can read, write, compute, and use technology to lead healthy, productive, and fulfilling lives.

ProLiteracy works with adult new readers and learners, and with local and national organizations to help adults gain the reading, writing, math, computer, and English skills they need to be successful in today's society. ProLiteracy advocates on behalf of adult learners and the programs that serve them, provides training and professional development, and publishes materials used in adult literacy instruction. It represents member programs in all 50 states and the District of Columbia, and in 50 developing countries.

ProLiteracy's publishing division, New Readers Press, develops and distributes literacy instructional products.

ProLiteracy

www.proliteracy.org
info@proliteracy.org

New Readers Press

www.newreaderspress.com
nrp@proliteracy.org

3

ACKNOWLEDGEMENTS

We Americans are all immigrants or descendants of immigrants—unless you're an American Indian. My grandparents came as teenagers to America from Sweden in the mid 1800s. They spoke only Swedish and had had limited education. Someone taught them to speak, understand, read, and write English. I'm grateful to those who helped them, and I hope that, in some small way, my teaching others "pays back" just a bit.

In 1972, Jane Root and I collaborated on the first edition of *Tutor*, a training guide for volunteers who wanted to work with adults who requested help in basic reading and writing. Over the next fifteen years, Jane and I reissued five more editions. In 1993, I worked with Judy Blankenship Cheatham and Lester L. Laminack to update the work in *Tutor*, 7th edition. I'll always be grateful to Jane Root, Judy Cheatham, and Lester Laminack for sharing their professional talents in such enthusiastic ways. Of course, we became good friends in the process.

This 8th edition of *Tutor* includes the best of all that has gone before as well as new material. I call your attention especially to a new chapter on Learning Disabilities and Learning Differences on which I worked closely with Corinne R. Smith at Syracuse University. How grateful I am to Dr. Smith for sharing her insights and her work! Her guidance has opened up ways to help those with special learning difficulties.

No work is ever done by one person, and *Tutor 8* is no exception. I'm indebted to all the students, tutors, trainers, program coordinators, and specialists in so many areas, who have over the years shared their stories and their expertise.

I do appreciate the help and suggestions given by reviewers of this 8th edition of *Tutor*: Mary Bartlett, Literacy New York; Judy Cheatham, Greensboro College, SC; Janice Cuddahee, Literacy New York; Jane Greiner, ProLiteracy Worldwide; Kathy Houghton, Literacy New York. For reviewing the chapter on Learning Disabilities and Learning Differences and adding practical suggestions, I want to thank: Rebecca Blangren, Greensboro College, SC; Linda Church, ProLiteracy Worldwide; Aggie Glavin, Learning Disabilities Association, Syracuse, NY; Jane Hugo, ProLiteracy Worldwide; Terry MacDonald, Syracuse University, NY; and Corinne Smith, Syracuse University. Thanks, too, to Chip Carlin, Literacy New York, for his suggestions on technology.

Special thanks to Beth Oddy, Managing Editor at New Readers Press, who kept me on the "straight and narrow," and to the staff at ProLiteracy who took care of all the necessary details that made this book possible.

My hope is that this book will give tutors and teachers the tools they need as they work to teach adults and teens basic reading and writing skills. It can be an "all win" situation. Students and learners will gain new skills, giving them opportunities to change their lives. Tutors and teachers will increase their skills as they teach, breaking down educational, cultural, racial, and economic barriers. And communities will gain as new relationships are formed to make stronger bonds within their borders. It can be a chain of helping hands—in communities, in cities and states, and even around the world.

I wish you all the joy I've had in making new friends as doors were opened—as I taught, as I did research, and as I shared ideas and concerns.

Ruth Colvin, Jan. 2009

4

CONTENTS

INTRODUCTION

THIS BOOK IS WRITTEN FOR ALL THOSE who are willing to expend their efforts to help adults who want to become better readers and writers.

Literacy Volunteers of America, now merged into ProLiteracy, grew out of a concern for the millions of people in the United States who speak and understand English but cannot read and write or whose reading and writing are so inadequate that their limited literacy is a problem in their everyday lives. Some did not profit from their school experiences. Some never had opportunities to attend school regularly. Others find their reading and writing skills insufficient for the demands of this changing world. Whatever the source of their problems, millions of people need your help learning to read and write.

ProLiteracy offers several training models in tutoring basic literacy. The training in *Tutor* is a professionally designed and field-tested workshop for the professional and non-professional reading and writing tutor. This text is designed to provide you with the following:

- a theoretical and attitudinal base from which to tutor
- demonstrations and discussions of needed skills and approaches for tutoring
- opportunities to practice these skills, which will be expanded during the training

Interwoven throughout the text and the training are five underlying themes that you will be putting into practice as you tutor:

1. respect for students as individuals
2. both tutors and students learning and teaching
3. sensitivity to adults' needs for immediate relevance
4. view of tutoring and learning as collaborative activities
5. integration of the four language components

In this text you will find professionally-accepted approaches and techniques with step-by-step instructions for tutoring basic literacy on a one-to-one basis, in a small group, or in a classroom setting. We generally use the terms *tutors*, *teachers*, *students*, and *learners* in the plural because we are referring to all tutors/teachers and all students/learners—whether the tutoring setting is one-to-one, a small group, or a classroom.

This book reflects more than four decades of experience, both volunteer and professional, with volunteer literacy programs. Techniques in teaching reading and writing have been adapted for the use of non-professional as well as professional tutors and teachers. Workable techniques explained in *Tutor* have emerged from a vital combination of practical experience and academically tested theory.

This text follows a holistic, integrated, collaborative, participating approach to understanding and teaching reading and writing, using Language Experience, sight words, phonics, and patterned words, always stressing comprehension, in a one-to-one, small group or classroom setting. The book is also designed to be used as a reference during lesson planning and tutoring.

Tutors should plan to attend additional in-service sessions provided by their local literacy programs, state literacy offices, Adult Basic Education programs, or other educational organizations in the community. Additional training is also available at ProLiteracy's annual conferences, which are open to students, tutors, trainers, administrative staff, and others interested in literacy.

This eighth version of *Tutor* assumes that you will do a great deal of reading, writing, listening, and speaking about each topic. One of our goals, in fact, is for you to use the book as a springboard to deepen your own understanding, to explore your assumptions, and to build your knowledge of literacy and tutoring. We encourage you to write in the margins, highlighting important ideas, making note of those things you find helpful and those things you want to come back to later.

One word about the case studies presented in these pages: these are all accounts of actual people. We have altered names and particular details of the situations to protect the confidentiality of those involved.

We invite you to join us and thousands of others across the country as together we work with people who have asked for help in reading and writing. As you help others, as you touch individual lives, you too will be touched. Your life will never be the same.

To learn, read
To know, write
To master, teach
oriental proverb

1

WHAT IS LITERACY?

Integration of Language Components
Listening – Speaking – Reading – Writing
Improving Lives Through Literacy
Examples of How Literacy Has Made a Difference
Real-Life Literacy

Reading: Philosophy and Approaches
Three Views of Reading
View One: Pronouncing Words
An Application of View One
View Two: Identifying and Defining Words
An Application of View Two
View Three: Bringing Meaning to the Text

Summary

HISTORICALLY, literacy has been defined by American culture in different ways: A hundred years ago literacy meant being able to sign one's name. Even today some people define literacy more precisely and narrowly than others. Some place the primary emphasis on reading; some define it as "spelling" or "printing" or "sounding out words;" some define it as the numbers of years in school. Advanced technology and an ever-changing world have expanded the skills and strategies needed to function successfully in our world and thus have expanded our nation's view of what it means to be "literate."

The National Literacy Act of 1991 defines literacy less narrowly, as "an individual's ability to read, write, and speak in English and compute and solve problems necessary to function on the job and in society, to achieve one's goals, and develop one's knowledge and potential." The National Center for Education Statistics (2003) defines literacy as "the ability to use printed and written information to function in society, to achieve one's goals, and to develop one's knowledge and potential." These definitions will no doubt be refined and changed, for social and cultural influences constantly call for redefining the terms.

Consider the everyday situations in which you use language to accomplish a variety of purposes. Some situations require you to receive information and make judgments; other situations demand that you express what you know to clarify your actions or involve others in the same activity. In either case you and other people are daily producers and consumers of language. The purpose of such interchanges is to understand, to communicate meaning.

INTEGRATION OF LANGUAGE COMPONENTS

Listening – Speaking – Reading – Writing

People often think of literacy as only reading and writing. Based both on experience and current research, ProLiteracy advocates that literacy instruction be viewed as involving all language components: listening, speaking, reading, and writing, as mediated through thought and with comprehension. We are advocating a balanced approach to teaching reading.

You may not have paid much attention to the roles of listening and speaking, considering only reading and writing as you think of literacy. Think about these facts:

- Linguists have identified over 6,000 languages. Perhaps half of these languages do not have written forms. In many cultures reading and writing are not language components, and so are not necessary for communication.

- The average baby hears language equivalent to a book a day from the primary caregiver. That baby begins to talk some time in the first two years after having heard the equivalent of 365 to 730 "novels." At about age four, five, or six, having been able to communicate quite nicely for several years, the child in a culture having written forms of language begins to learn to read and write.

Reading and writing, in our culture, are as important and vital ways of communicating as are listening and speaking.

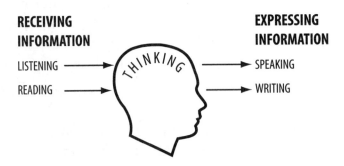

Listening and reading are two channels for receiving information; speaking and writing are two channels for expressing information. Reading and writing are communicated through written symbols; listening and speaking, through oral symbols. Reading, writing, listening, speaking—all require the individual to think, to engage in the process of expressing or receiving information.

If we separate reading from writing and listening from speaking, we simply fragment language. In short, we unnecessarily complicate matters, making language learning much more difficult than it needs to be. And if we further divide reading into a series of separate skills {sounds, vocabulary exercises, syllabification, affixes, and prefixes), we continue to make reading seem less and less a part of natural language. For that reason, we present language as an integrated whole and believe that language teaching needs to integrate all the language components. This philosophy of language instruction is sometimes referred to as whole language. It could also be called complete language, for it includes all four components of language—listening, speaking, reading, and writing—and emphasizes comprehension.

Improving Lives Through Literacy

Literacy is never meant to be taught in isolation. It can change lives, enabling people to address broader social issues—in individual lives, in families, in the workplace, and in communities. Literacy issues are basic to health issues, to incarceration issues, to immigration issues, to workplace issues, to all of life. We suggest using authentic or real life reading materials, making reading more relevant to the students' real life issues and introducing them to problem solving techniques.

Raising literacy levels is important, but just as important and more meaningful are the outcomes that result from learning to read and write, outcomes that empower individuals to make changes in their lives, in their workplaces, and in their communities.

Tutor focuses on basic skills, critical thinking, and learner-initiated action to attain learner-centered goals. These goals could be related to health, employment, environment, safety, or might focus on wider concerns for peace and human rights. New readers can be empowered and given the confidence to solve their own problems and to reach out to others when help is needed.

All the reading and writing techniques described in *Tutor* can be applied to materials of interest and concern to individual students. Reading newspapers, filling out job applications, keeping grocery lists, using a calendar to remind one of appointments, reading a manual from the workplace—all give practice and confidence to struggling students as they face these tasks daily. You'll read student stories throughout *Tutor* that tell how literacy skills changed adults' lives, empowering them to make decisions and take action.

Examples of How Literacy Has Made a Difference

In an Individual Life • Lorna Fenner, a low-level reader, had six children. She admitted she had never been able to read to her older children, but learning to read made it possible for her to read her older daughter's report card and understand that Tina had failed the math Regents exam.

Being able to read and write gave Lorna the courage to write first to her daughter's teacher, then to the principal, insisting her daughter get special help. Nothing was available except repeating the class. This didn't stop Lorna. She called her tutor. Did she know anyone who could help her daughter in math? After passing the request along to friends, the tutor found a teenage boy, Marty, who had aced the math Regents. With Marty's mother's consent, the boy agreed to tutor Tina at the local library. No, she didn't pass the first retest, but she did pass the second one. Tina is now a freshman in college, something that would never have happened if Lorna had not learned to read and write, getting the courage and self confidence to search for help.

In the Workplace • Max, Kenny, and José worked as a team in a fast food restaurant. They knew their routine jobs, and things were going well. When a new work manual arrived, they were frustrated and concerned for their jobs. They tried to read the manual, to understand how it would affect their jobs, but it made little sense to them. Why couldn't it have been written more simply so they could understand it? What to do?

Kenny suggested they write a letter to their boss, asking for help in understanding what this meant for their specific jobs. Not one of the men felt confident in his writing, but José suggested they go together to their literacy teacher and ask for help. Together they wrote the letter, and the boss explained in simpler terms. The letter led to the fast food company rewriting the manual in words that their workers could understand.

In a Neighborhood/Community • Neighbors in a poor section of town learned that a drug dealer was working in a nearby house. They tried calling the police, but finally realized that they would have to write a letter, petitioning the mayor and other city officials to close the house. None of the neighbors felt competent enough in writing to write the note, but Joshua decided he'd take the responsibility of getting their problem on paper. His teacher had shown him how to "map," that is, jot down everyone's ideas, giving him the basic outline of what the group wanted to say.

Their combined effort, with Joshua writing down their complaints, brought the problem to the attention of the officials. Joshua and his neighbors used Joshua's reading and writing skills to get the officials to shut down the drug dealer in their neighborhood.

Through literacy lessons, changes are being made in situations where students feel empowered and take action to solve their problems—in individual lives, in workplace settings, and in communities.

Real-Life Literacy

If you cannot read Greek, this want ad will be incomprehensible to you.

ΜΑΓΕΙΡΙΣΣΑ Καλδζ
Ευεφγετηματα
Απο 8 Π.Μ. εωζ 3 Μ.Μ.
Τηλεφωυηοατε 429–3610

This same ad in English is just as incomprehensible to a non-reader of English.

Wanted: COOK
Good Pay—Benefits
Hours: 8 am-3 pm
Call: 429-3610

Put yourself in the place of a non-reading homemaker. Imagine how frustrating it would be not to be able to read directions on a brownie mix box!

EASY BROWNIE DIRECTIONS

HEAT	oven to 350°
GREASE	bottom only of a 13 x 9 inch pan.
MIX	brownie mix, 1/2 cup oil, 1 cup lukewarm water, and 2 eggs in a large bowl. Stir vigorously with fork for 50 strokes. Spread mixture into pan.
BAKE	28 minutes or until toothpick inserted in center comes out clean.

Think of the things that could happen if you were not able to read signs such as these:

Suppose you were a parent with a sick child and you could not read the labels on a medicine bottle?

One maintenance worker smoked his cigarette behind the tank that had the following signs, having no idea of the potential disaster he could cause.

In each situation, literacy is a part of, not separate from, life.

Literacy helps us to remember, to organize ideas, to prove our points, to make judgments, to eat wisely, to save money, to care for our children, to improve and maintain health, to entertain ourselves, to assemble and repair products, to prepare for discussions, to broaden our views, to improve or increase efficiency at home or at work, and to be full participants in society.

READING: PHILOSOPHY AND APPROACHES

Everyone seems to agree that the ultimate purpose of reading is to arrive at meaning. However, we can identify at least three basic views of learning to read, each of which places a different emphasis on the role of meaning. Your personal definition of reading will probably fit into one of these three broad perspectives:

- *View One:* Learning to read means learning to pronounce words.
- *View Two:* Learning to read means learning to identify words and get their meanings.
- *View Three:* Learning to read means learning to bring meaning to a text in order to understand it (Weaver, 1988).

As a learner-centered literacy program, ProLiteracy subscribes to View Three.

Three Views of Reading

To illustrate these three definitions, we will use the following diagram.

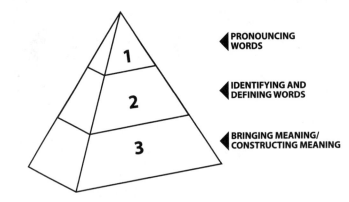

Let's examine each view.

View One: Pronouncing Words

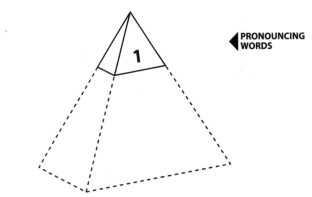

Learning to read, in this view, means learning to pronounce words. The basic focus is to teach students the names of letters and to train students to give the sound(s) associated with each letter. Associating letters with sounds is called letter-sound correspondence. Training in letter-sound correspondence is usually followed by more instruction in blending letters or in learning rules for combining the letters and sounds to produce words.

Words may be introduced slowly and are usually only those words that fit the letter-sound correspondences taught thus far. In some cases, lists of words comprised of the letter-sound pairings already taught are developed for the students to drill. Words from these lists are often combined into short passages.

View One is important but limited. Rarely do contrived passages consist of language natural to the ears of the students or the tutors. Furthermore, merely pronouncing a word will never give a reader meaning if he or she has never seen or heard the word.

An Application of View One

Suppose you suddenly found yourself able to use only the skills of View One. Suppose you could say all the words printed on a page but had no idea what they meant. To understand the limitations of View One, try the passage below:

MAS GRAN!

The gleb xupped in the middle of the zee. Jim pabbed, "Watash! I'm out of sieg!"

"Frong down, Jim," parla his esop. 'The parta won't blad because we're out of sieg!"

"You're tost," pabbed Jim. "Let's tig the zee on min!"

So the two breeks tigged the zee on min!

Comprehension Check:
1. What did the gleb do?
2. Where were Jim and the esop?
3. What wouldn't blad?
4. Why wouldn't it?
5. What did the two breeks do?

Skills Check:
1. What is the subject of sentence one? What is the verb?
2. What tense is *pabbed?* How do you know?
3. Make *zee* plural.
4. Make *breeks* singular.
5. Draw a line between the subject and the predicate in the last sentence.

Were you able to say all the words? Were you able to answer the questions correctly? Could you identify the parts of speech? Can you explain or retell the story? Can you define the "new" words? Suppose you knew that "zee" was a type of road and "gleb" was a particular model of car. Now re-read the passage. What a difference a context makes!

View Two: Identifying and Defining Words

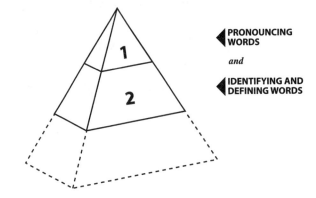

Learning to read, in this view, means learning to identify words and understand their meaning.

The second view of reading incorporates View One, since knowing some letter-sound correspondences can be useful in identifying words. This point of view is concerned with the correct pronunciation of words paired with the ability to define them or use them in sentences. In this view, the major focus of learning to read is to build the number of words students can identify and to increase the students' collection of individual word meanings.

This view assumes that the readers' ability to say the words in print and to use those words in sentences (or to give definitions of those words) automatically leads to the building of an understanding of the material in which those words occur. It holds that the entire passage will be understood if, prior to reading, the new words for the lesson are presented.

View Two is also important but limited. These materials may have little or no connection to the learners' life experiences, interests, or needs. The language may be artificial, awkward, or contrived; it may not be the natural language of the students.

An Application of View Two

Have you ever been able to "read" and understand the meaning of every single word in a passage, but when you were finished, have no clue as to what you have just read? You found yourself merely calling words.

Read through the following list of words:

in	four	methods	for
common	use	the	evaluating
cooling	of	quenching	mediums
are	power	basic	test
magnetic	curve	hot	interval
wire	and		

1. Are there words you cannot read?
2. Are there any words you cannot define?

Chances are that you can read and define all but a few of these words. You might think that you would be prepared to read these same words in the context of a written passage. Read the following:

> Four methods in common use for evaluating the cooling power of quenching mediums are the basic cooling curve test, the interval test, the hot wire test, and the magnetic test. (*Metals Handbook,* 8th edition, "Heat Treating, Cleaning and Finishing" page 18 – American Society for Metals)

Would you be able to retell this passage in your own words, explaining how to use the information?

Chances are that you could not. That's not an unusual response; many readers would find it difficult. The difficulty lies not in the words or in their meanings—for we can read these words and we generally know what they mean. The difficulty lies in the very specific subject of the passage—treatment of metals Without a background in the treatment of metals, a reader is not going to be able to make much sense of the passage.

Unfortunately, the ability to read words at a glance and to define these words does not ensure comprehension. This exercise should help us all recognize how frustrated adult new readers may feel when they spend weeks reviewing letters, sounds, and words in isolation with the promise of comprehension once they begin to read "real" materials. Then they pick up a menu, a magazine, the newspaper, only to find that reading those items is not like sounding out words, reading a word list or words out of context.

View Three: Bringing Meaning to the Text

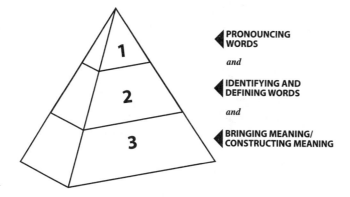

In View Three, learning to read means learning to bring meaning to the words in a text in order to get meaning from or to understand the text.

The primary emphasis of View Three is on building meaning, on comprehension. View Two extends the original pyramid because it includes View One. By the same token, View Three creates the broad base for this same pyramid, encompassing both View One and View Two. View Three recognizes that readers use their knowledge of language and their general knowledge of the world to build personally relevant meaning from the language of the writer. This process involves use of the various strategies and skills to be presented in this book.

The difference between this third view and the first two views, however, is that in the first two, reading is either an act of learning letters and sounds or a linear process of learning to recognize words and recall their meanings. In contrast, View Three presents reading as an active, dynamic, human process that involves using all that people know about the world and their own language to make sense of new information in print. View Three incorporates Views One and Two and is the view that ProLiteracy advocates. It serves as a foundation for the approaches you will learn to use in this book.

From this view of literacy, tutoring material includes any print students need or want to read. It could be newspaper articles, ads, job announcements, manuals, personal or business letters, children's books, literature, religious material, menus, letters, the phone book, or stories the learners have written. Most importantly, material is taken from the interests and backgrounds of the students. The material is not predetermined with language made to fit a vocabulary list or the sound of a particular letter.

Since these materials are authentic or real life (e.g., a newspaper rather than a workbook designed to look like a newspaper), the resulting tutoring session is "adult." In it, people use language (read, write, talk, and listen) with real materials. Furthermore, if the tutoring material reflects a student's special interest and expertise, then that student is recognized as the expert on the topic. This may mean that while we might read words with learners, they each will be able and expected to explain to us what has been read.

It does not mean that workbooks that focus on sound-symbols, that focus on whole words, that focus on other parts of language should not be included in the lessons. They are important and should be included, especially in early lessons. Students learn in different ways, and tutors should be aware of what works best with their students. Seldom does "one size fit all."

View Three, however, is the most useful for a literacy tutor because it respects students' cultures and languages and validates their reasons for wanting to learn. This view allows students to be central in the process by which they learn to read.

SUMMARY

Think of the process of learning to read and write as a continuous, ongoing act expanding itself as readers/writers interact with the world of print. Print situations—where reading can occur—happen everywhere, not just in special materials written for the purpose of "teaching someone to read and write." In the same way, writing occurs in real-life, everyday situations.

We want to demonstrate to students that learning to read and write means learning to create and understand meaning. Learning to read and write is more than moving through grade levels and filling out worksheets to show mastery of the proper skills. As tutors, we all need to validate the literacy events our students engage in daily.

LEARNING AND TUTORING

ALL HUMAN BEINGS are at one time or another both students and teachers. When it is your turn to "teach" you must respect your students as human beings fully worthy and deserving of human dignity. As tutors, you must respect students' rights to

- hold views different from your own;
- have language patterns that do not match yours or the dominant culture's;
- have goals different from the goals you might choose for them.

In essence, you want to treat students as you yourself like to be treated when the roles are reversed in life. This book uses "student" and "learner" interchangeably. The terms are not as important as the concept. The book is not, then, trying to make a social or linguistic statement when using one term or the other. All people are students and teachers, learners and facilitators, in various situations in life. Both roles require mutual respect.

HOW DO WE LEARN?

Learning is a natural human activity. We learn because we're human. It is in our nature to learn, to try to figure things out, to think, to wonder. We do it with varying degrees of success, but we all learn. What we learn, however, depends on various factors.

We learn most things in life because we are part of the demonstrations constantly going on around us. Remember the proverb:

> Tell me and I will forget.
> Show me and I will remember.
> Let me do and I will understand.

Learning does not take place in isolation. *Literacy* learning is a collaboration between students and tutors working together as partners to reach a common goal, to complete a common task. We are all learners together, students and tutors.

Even as you tutor, you will be constantly learning. Perhaps you will learn more about how people become literate; perhaps you will learn more about the goals of your students. By assisting in the pursuit of those goals through relevant material, you might even learn about plumbing, landscaping, midwifery, or children's literature. Also, as you admit your lack of knowledge on various topics, your students may realize that they have something to teach you as well.

Students are often good problem solvers, having skills that tutors may not. Tutors can often learn about their students' abilities by listening to how they have coped with not being able to read and write in a reading and writing society. This pooling of knowledge and skills is something both will learn to do more of as tutoring sessions progress successfully.

In the last forty years, a great deal has been discovered about how people learn. However, good teachers, both in and out of formal school situations, have been around much longer than forty years. Each of you probably has been fortunate enough to have had at least one person you can look to as a role model as you go through your training and into your tutoring sessions. Even though you will most likely be tutoring using approaches and techniques that differ from those you remember being taught with, aspiring to these qualities of an effective teacher/tutor will stand you in good stead.

LEARNING STYLES

People learn in a variety of ways. One of your jobs as a teacher is to find the ways your students learn best. How do you find your students' best learning styles? Find clues from their learning differences.

A famous surgeon told the story that while in school he wasn't doing well on his exams although he attended all his classes and worked hard. He realized he wasn't "getting it" through the lectures, so instead he concentrated on *reading* the books, rather than on depending on the lectures. He "got it." He realized that he had to learn *how* he learned. He was not an auditory learner; he was a visual learner.[1]

- Are your students visual learners? Do they learn best through their eyes, through seeing, reading, or visualizing things?
- Or is the auditory approach, hearing through their ears, their best way to learn?
- Or perhaps they learn best by having things modeled for them, asking questions, paraphrasing what was said or read, even making lists or drawing pictures to help them remember, things they can feel or touch.
- Yet others learn better by actually doing, trying out for themselves.

Most of us use a combination of a variety of learning styles.

A simple way to find out is to ask your students what works best for them when being directed to a specific destination. You're going to give directions in several ways.

- First, you'll show a map and point to the starting spot, then follow along the route to the final destination. A visual learner prefers that way.
- Second, you'll tell them where the starting point is, tell directions by saying "go straight for two blocks, turn left and go straight for three blocks, turn right, and there is your destination." An auditory learner finds this best.
- Third, you'll show the map and give oral directions, but you find your students must question and paraphrase your directions, sometimes writing themselves notes. These students have to reframe the information to "get it."
- Fourth, some students find they learn better if they actually walk or drive the route. They have to actually do it themselves to learn best.

---

[1] Dr. Ben Carson, neurosurgeon at John Hopkins in *Take the Risk: Learning to Identify, Choose, and Live with Acceptable Risk,* Zondervan, 2008

What does this mean for reading? Visual learners will want to look at the whole word, guess at it using the story's content, and then sound out the word. Auditory learners prefer to sound out words. The reframing learner may prefer for you to model reading a sentence first, then they respond. The "do it" reader may prefer to plunge right in, with you giving corrective feedback as needed.

Some students are "impulsive," while others are "reflective." Impulsive students usually leave off word endings, don't recheck their work and often guess, taking little time to problem solve because they think they've "got it." Reflective students are constantly sounding out, analyzing, checking and double checking, often missing the main point or even the whole word. Many have a slower learning pace, plodding along, learning eventually, if you have patience and give them enough time. Others have the ability to learn through observation, while still others have keen intuitions. Yet others must be guided every inch of the way. Some have memory problems but others have outstanding memories.

Some students learn best when focusing on the big picture (they see the forest) while others learn best when focusing on details (they see the trees). Some like to work independently while others prefer interaction with others. Some students answer questions immediately, often guessing or giving intuitive answers, while others do better when taking more time to think through their answers. Many adult students want practical knowledge using real objects or life examples, while others are more comfortable in a fantasy or make-believe world.

It's important to be sensitive to your students' learning styles, but also to be aware of your own style of teaching and learning. We, as tutors and teachers, have dominant *teaching* styles, preferred ways to teach. Some of us feel it's best to give the big picture, the overall view of a lesson first, and are impatient with details. Others find they prefer to start with sequential steps, one step logically following the other, keeping things orderly, paying attention to detail. Some of us like to put examples in writing for our students to see. Others prefer to read instructions and examples, feeling hearing is more effective. Some teachers may use a responsive, collaborative, learner-directed way of teaching, while others are more comfortable with a more controlling, teacher-directed way. Both learner-directed and teacher-directed approaches can be effective, and many teachers practice an eclectic approach incorporating elements of both. How teachers approach learning situations affects how students learn. In this instance, because of the learning challenges of many of our students, we, as teachers, may need to suspend our own styles in the best interests of the learners.

We all learn in a variety of ways, and we all have preferred ways of learning. Whatever the teaching and learning styles of tutors and students, learning is most effective when sensitive and careful planning, a willingness to adapt, and enthusiasm and patience are a part of each session. Some will learn more easily if they can *see* or *feel* what is to be learned. Other learners may have to *hear* it to know it. Some students prefer to guide the material toward their interests. Others always ask to be given the answer, because this helps them understand more deeply. When planning lessons, it is important for you to know that different people have different preferred styles of learning. You will learn several ways to teach, and there is no easy way to predict what will work best for a particular student. You will need to experiment, observe carefully, and then use what works.

HOW DO WE TUTOR READING?

Think about teaching done daily in real-life situations. Think about teaching a friend to knit or hang wallpaper, or teaching a teenager to drive a car. You don't have a book that tells you how to teach, a year's worth of lesson plans, and an outline of what is to be taught and when. So how do you do it?

You approach the students with respect. You begin by discussing the students' expectations. You provide many demonstrations. You usually show and/or tell your students what needs to be done. When it's the students' turn to "do," you usually assist, to the extent assistance is needed and welcomed, withdrawing your help if you see it is not. Then, after a while, the students do it on their own. This way, the students develop independence and responsibility while recognizing the tutor's role as coach/facilitator. The expectation is that the students will learn what is being taught.

Remember, in View Three of reading, the emphasis is on building meaning. This is done by using the learners' personal knowledge of a topic, their ability to construct the meaning of words in the context of a specific situation, and their ability to employ various strategies including word knowledge and letter-sound correspondence as needed to understand what is being read and written.

Learning and tutoring take place most readily in a collaborative working situation of mutual respect and shared expectations for success. As tutors, you will learn to use mutually determined goals, to negotiate what happens in a lesson, and to encourage self-assessment on your part as well as your students'.

How do adult learners look at their new tutors? What do they expect? How do new tutors feel as they meet with adult basic literacy students? How you relate to your students as people is as important as the reading and writing learning processes you will be promoting.

WHO ARE ADULT LEARNERS?

Think of the factors in your own life that have helped or hindered you when you entered into a formal learning situation. How did you work out the details? What kind of help and encouragement did you need just to make the decision? What things discouraged you? What things encouraged you? In what ways do you think the adults you'll be working with will be similar to you? In what ways do you expect them to be different?

In the context of *Tutor*, adult learners are those adults who need and want help in improving their proficiencies in basic reading and writing.

Characteristics of Most Adult Learners

As a tutor, you should be aware of the characteristics of adult learners. You may find that you share some of these same attributes as you go through new learning experiences yourself, such as this training. No one adult tutor or student has all the characteristics listed, but reviewing them may help you to be aware of them as you clarify goals and plan individual lessons.

There is no typical adult learner. Adult literacy programs have both male and female students whose ages may range from 16 to 80 plus. The student population reflects the general population. Students come from various ethnic, religious, and economic backgrounds and may represent all the possible family structures existing in the community. School experience will range from none to twelve or more years. Some hold responsible jobs, while others are unemployed. Some have stable home lives while others are burdened with social problems. But two things are certain: they want to improve their reading and writing, and they need your help.

Adult Learners Are Creative and Adaptable • The inability to read and write does not necessarily indicate a lack of intelligence. Many nonreaders are intelligent and creative in finding ways to compensate for their lack of proficiency in literacy. As one student commented, "I don't have trouble thinking. My trouble is just reading."

Adult students differ from children in many ways, especially in their range of life experiences. Personality, habits, attitudes, and interests have solidified to a far greater degree than in children, sometimes making adults comparatively more rigid and less receptive to change. But most adults know better what they want from educational encounters, have rich personal experiences on which to build, and can be motivated to try different approaches.

Adult learners are not blank slates. They, like all other students, have had failures. However, they also have unique talents and have had successes in some areas of life—family, church, neighborhood, or job. They simply do not have the strategies for reading and writing that they need and want. They need to be encouraged to use the adaptability and creativity they have demonstrated in other areas of their lives to develop greater proficiency with reading and writing.

Adult Learners Feel Apprehensive or Anxious • Basic literacy students, like other adults going into new ventures, may very well face the experience with much hesitancy and apprehension. They may be thinking: "Am I capable of learning after all these years? Can you teach an old dog new tricks? I've failed so many times. Will this be another failure? Will my friends find out?"

Some adults do not show up for the first meeting with the tutor. Sometimes, on reflection, they decide not to go through with the lessons. Sometimes an unexpected problem arises, such as the sickness of a child. Or perhaps the problem is with transportation. There are also adults who have trouble facing new experiences; the unknown can be very frightening. It takes a great deal of courage to admit needs and to ask for assistance, and some adults cannot muster the courage to attend the first meeting.

What about you? You are the tutor. You have been trained to teach and have been told about your students in advance. Do you think you will have butterflies in your stomach when you go to your first tutoring session? Think how much more frightening this experience can be for students who have little, if any, awareness of what to expect.

Adults Are Uneven Learners • Because of each adult's unique history and experience, learning cycles may be unpredictable and uneven throughout your teaching sessions.

Have you ever had a day when you could do nothing wrong, only to have it followed by a day when you could do nothing right? This up-and-down, uneven pace is natural to all learning. Some days, your students may learn quite easily, and you will feel a buoyancy about your progress. But at other times, cues will be missed, reading will drag, and writing just will not flow. You may feel a particular student is not trying, especially if a forgetful or dull day follows a good one.

Uneven learning results from the nature of the learners and from the task itself. Don't be too upset with yourself or your learners if an occasional lesson seems unproductive. Your students may be able to do some things you think are quite complex and at the same time not be able to do things you consider simple.

Adult Learners Want Lessons to be Relevant to Their Lives • We must remember that we are working with adults who have survived and succeeded mostly beyond their reading/writing abilities. They have probably not been called on to "study" for some time, but are willing to follow your lead, hoping that these lessons will help them in their daily lives. They're willing to work on sub-skills, such as phonics or sight word cards, but their goal is to make these skills relevant to their goals and lives.

So keep in mind the practical needs of your students. Let them know that the sub-skills learned will eventually lead to attaining their goals.

Adult Learners Need Support, Reassurance, and Praise • Human beings respond positively to frequent praise and reassurance. Students need to be constantly reminded that they are progressing, that they are learning, that they are becoming independent readers and writers. Don't be patronizing, giving undeserved compliments. But do give praise for even little goals attained. A smile, a "well done," and other words of encouragement go a long way to encourage students to keep on trying, especially after a difficult lesson.

Adult Learners Have Outside Responsibilities • Like all adults, nonreaders sometimes have problems not directly related to their inability to read and write. Some have domestic difficulties that cause them to have feelings of hopelessness. Their problems, like yours, are varied and sometimes serious. However, they must face these problems without the ease of access to information that literacy provides.

If students are disturbed by a sick child, a lost job, or domestic difficulties, they may find it difficult to concentrate on reading and writing. You cannot solve all their problems, but you can listen, ask constructive questions, and perhaps direct them to the appropriate agencies. You can also use these home situations as the source of writing and reading materials for instruction.

Many people who do not read or write are able to cope with life to their own satisfaction. They might trade off their practical skills with others who do their reading and writing for them. They are usually part of a family, neighborhood, work, or religious network and have other responsibilities to deal with in addition to attending tutoring sessions. As they increase their proficiencies with reading and writing, their places in their networks often change. These changes may be positive, or they may become obstacles which will have to be dealt with.

Even time scheduled for lessons and home study may vary since all adult learners have lives with various commitments outside the literacy lessons. Most have responsibilities for the basic needs of their families, often necessitating overtime work or second jobs.

Adult Learners May Have Learning Disabilities, Learning Differences • Many of our adult learners have a history of learning problems. Many were put in special classes or were told they were "stupid" or "lazy." Yes, they have learning difficulties, learning differences, but they are asking for our help. Chapter 10 discusses learning disabilities and learning differences with suggestions for how you can help these students.

Additional Characteristics • Adult learners generally view themselves as responsible, self-directed, and independent, preferring to make their own decisions. They resent being treated like children and often feel threatened by formal tests. Many adult students are impatient regarding their own progress which may present challenges since their learning is often uneven or erratic. Some will enjoy reading for pleasure and writing about their own experiences; for others, however, the most immediate needs will be for practical lessons that will satisfy their personal goals. Most adults seem to learn better in informal settings.

Of course, not all these characteristics apply to all adult learners, but being sensitive to your students' experiences and expectations will help you create a relaxed atmosphere as you plan together.

Your students may wonder what you are getting out of the tutoring experience. When they find that you are a volunteer—that you are teaching because you sincerely care and want to help—a new understanding of the collaborative tutoring partnership often results.

Summary—Characteristics of Adult Learners

Most adult learners

- are creative and adaptable
- feel apprehensive or anxious
- learn unevenly
- want lessons to be relevant to their lives
- need support, reassurance, and praise
- have outside responsibilities
- view themselves as responsible, self-directed, independent
- prefer to make their own decisions
- resent being treated like children
- feel threatened by formal tests
- want practical lessons that satisfy personal goals
- have had varied life experiences
- may have learning disabilities, learning differences

WHAT MAKES AN EFFECTIVE BASIC LITERACY TUTOR/TEACHER?

The desire to help and the willingness to give time to tutoring are indispensable but not enough. Learning the strategies and techniques of teaching basic reading and writing—including how to assess learners' strengths, needs, interests, and goals, and how to plan lessons based upon that ongoing assessment—is essential to effective tutoring.

Effective teachers usually have several characteristics in common. As you begin to tutor, look for those characteristics in your own tutoring. Some of the skills you already have will help you to gain the new skills and strategies that you will need. Some of these are technical, the "how-to" skills, but others are based on personal qualities such as patience, understanding, and enthusiasm.

It's important for tutors to demonstrate their love and need for reading and writing. Share the reading and writing that you are doing, whether it's for pleasure, for information, or for work. Let your students know that reading and writing are lifelong skills that continue to open doors for all of us.

Characteristics of Effective Tutors

Learner-Centeredness • Learner-centered tutoring is directly related to the learners' needs and goals. It means keeping students at the heart of instruction and seeing students as equal partners in the learning process. Your students are entitled to know why certain techniques or strategies are important. Discussing why you are concentrating on a specific activity shows that you recognize your students' abilities to think and reason. They need to gain personal skills, not to see a demonstration of the skills you possess. The tutor must show how, not show off.

Patience • Sometimes learning seems very slow. It takes time for everything to jell, and you might get discouraged: "What am I doing wrong? We've met for a month, and my student can't read or write." Think about yourself. Did you learn to read and write in one month? Did you quit trying because you didn't? Of course not. Expect success, keep encouraging, and above all be patient—with the learners and with yourself. Remember, you are very close to the learning situation. Your student may have made more progress than you realize.

Understanding and Respect • Basic to all teaching is a respect for your students. Try to understand their situations. Most students have already faced many social problems, some of which relate to their low literacy ability. You cannot solve all their problems. You can, however, try to be understanding as you work with them.

Many students have covered up their limited skills for so long that they're often hesitant to expose their needs. Respect your students' desires for confidentiality. On the other hand, if some students want to extend themselves into new areas using their new skills, respect this and support them.

Creativity • Your creativity is important. You will find yourself adapting successful techniques suggested by others, as well as ideas you've found helpful in other situations. You and your students will be directing the course of study together, based on a solid understanding of what all of you are doing.

Asking you to be creative in tutoring reading and writing would not be fair if you had no base of knowledge. *Tutor* and the accompanying Basic Literacy Tutor Training Workshop provide the basic approaches, techniques, and knowledge about tutoring and learning that will allow you to apply your creativity. Adapt these basics to your students' needs and abilities.

Sensitivity • Some learners have bluffed their way along for many years, using their wits to cover up their reading and writing weaknesses. It may be very hard for these adults or teenagers to admit that they have difficulty accomplishing tasks often expected of children. Compensating behavior, like pretending to know, is hard to change, but as the relationship between you and your students develops and brings about mutual trust, these lifelong defensive habits will become less necessary. Be gentle with these learners.

A good tutor offers students clues to make success possible. Hearing "no" too often is as discouraging as being interrupted too often. If your students are puzzled or discouraged in their reading or writing, be ready to change your lesson plans. Be sensitive to your students' actions and reactions at all times.

Paying attention to students' problems is important in easing the tension in their lives and retaining them in the program. If you find a situation in which you feel uncomfortable or untrained, remember you are not expected to be a counselor, therapist, or social worker. You should contact your literacy program for guidance in referring that student to the appropriate agency for assistance. Dealing with problems in this way will show your concern while not asking you for skills and training you might not possess.

Be sensitive to differences in life styles, cultural backgrounds, and formal education. Remember that learning acquired in the school of life is valid and valuable. Respect your students' rich life experiences.

Realistic Expectations • Sometimes tutors are unrealistic in what they think their students can accomplish. Often dreams and idealism lead to outstanding performance. But tutors must realize that some of the students with literacy problems have other problems as well, for example, learning differences or an unwillingness or an inability to give sessions the time and concentration needed. Tutors must be realistic and aware of what their students can reasonably accomplish. Focus on what goes well and on what the students can do. Sometimes your students may have realistic goals but unrealistic timetables. Without an honest approach, both tutors and students can become frustrated, disillusioned, and discouraged. A blend of idealism and reality is the goal.

Empathy • In order to be supportive, you must empathize with your students. Let your students know that you will be supportive even when things aren't going as planned. Each of us needs to know that someone else has confidence in us and will stick with us, helping and encouraging.

Sense of Humor • A tough task is often made easier by including some light moments. Laughter often reduces tension. A good joke read or shared is a fine way to build a relationship and add pleasure to some otherwise hard work. An instructional hour with several laughs in it will seem like a much shorter time. Tutors who can laugh at their own occasional mistakes can usually ease the tension when learners make mistakes. Be genuine, though, and beware of sarcasm. Sarcasm is always destructive.

Adaptability • People are infinitely different. Some have phenomenal memories. Some have keen intuition. Some have a knack of learning through observation. Some are plodders who will learn eventually if you have patience enough to allow them the time. Your job is to adapt your tutoring to your students' interests and abilities and to their styles of learning. Be open-minded to new ideas and a variety of teaching techniques.

Enthusiasm • Keep your enthusiasm high, giving genuine encouragement to your students so they will feel a sense of accomplishment with each success, no matter how small. Many small successes must occur before any long-term success can be achieved. Do not pretend success when both you and your students know it has not been attained. While excessive pressure and urging are not conducive to learning, genuine respect and regard for your students' growth are sources of help, pride, and motivation.

Organizational Skills • As a tutor, you are responsible for planning lessons and working with your students to set goals. Unfortunately, there will never seem to be enough time for everything you anticipate doing. Therefore you should try to do two things:

- First, extend your tutoring session by planning between-session activities, or home practice, which will give your students practice in both reading and writing.
- Second, focus your sessions on the purpose of the lesson.

You are responsible for working with your learners, showing up on time, observing and assessing how they are doing, planning the lessons, demonstrating/modeling, encouraging, maintaining records, and reporting to your literacy office. Because your main job is to help your students grow in reading, writing, and comprehension skills, each session with your students must be a tutoring session.

You need to pay special attention to your conversation. Of course you want to be friendly and personable with your students, but small talk shouldn't interfere with the purpose of the lesson. In addition, some adults may use chatty conversation to avoid the task because they feel unprepared or anxious. You may suggest that you use the first five minutes or perhaps the last few minutes to catch up on personal conversation; on the other hand, you will have to decide when a listening friend is needed. Use your own good judgment.

Commitment • Success stories are encouraging, but not all students will be successful. Teenage and adult nonreaders are on the lower steps of a ladder, and that next step up is often very big. Some may never take it. Working with their own tutors is the last hope for many adults. You are encouraged not to give up before you have abundant evidence that there will not be enough progress to sustain the gains in proficiency. Check with your program coordinator to see if a focus on survival skills for a short period of time would be appropriate.

As you move to help someone learn to read and write better, remember that positive personal qualities and knowledge about learning and tutoring are needed. The fact that you have chosen to try to help someone shows that you are motivated.

Summary—Characteristics of Effective Tutors

Effective tutors

- are learner-centered
- have patience
- are understanding and respectful
- are creative
- are sensitive
- have realistic expectations

- have empathy
- have a sense of humor
- are adaptable
- have enthusiasm
- have organizational skills
- have commitment

COLLABORATIVE TUTORING SESSIONS

The process of collaborative tutoring is the same whether you are teaching one-to-one, in a small group of three to five, or in a class. You are a team or partnership of people working together to accomplish the same goal. The tutor/teacher facilitates learning but also learns as part of the team or group. The structure, elements, or steps of the collaborative session are also the same. The differences in these situations are in the interactions either between two people or among a group of people. As you work with your student, small group, or class, you might want to anticipate the stages of development.

Changing Relationships

The relationship between two people or among the members of a small group or a class changes with time as the participants work together. These stages of change are somewhat predictable, and understanding them can help you adjust your style and role to support learning success.

The following discussion of the stages through which a one-to-one, small group, or classroom relationship progresses is based on "Tuckman's Model of Group Process," by B. W. Tuckman and M. A. C. Jensen (1977) (see Appendix, page 200).

The stages suggested are in order: forming, storming, norming, performing, and adjourning.

1. **Forming**   As the group forms, the students expect the tutor to take the lead in planning lessons, setting goals, and setting up rules for the group.

2. **Storming**   As individuals within the group grow more independent, there might be resistance to the tutor taking total leadership. They may question the value of some of the techniques and materials. This indicates growth and shows that it is time for students to assume more responsibilities.

3. **Norming**   As a group works closely together, a sense of cooperation and a greater sense of unity usually develop. Individual personalities emerge, and decision-making by the students becomes more evident. They become less dependent on the tutor for guidance.

4. **Performing** Lessons have become more relaxed, with tutors and students accepting each other, working together, and taking responsibility for decision making. There is a sense of accomplishment and satisfaction as skills of speaking, listening and understanding, reading, and writing are integrated into meaningful tasks.

5. **Adjourning** Eventually the tutoring must end. Adjourning should not be done abruptly. Time should be allowed for affirmations, for sadness at parting, and for closure. Perhaps a final celebration session can be planned where certificates are given or students share their best work over the year. Perhaps the students will want to plan a final meeting over lunch or coffee. Parting will be easier for the students if they know they can continue to call their tutor and each other for help or encouragement, or just to keep in touch.

It is important to keep in mind that the stages identified by Tuckman and Jensen are only a model. Although actual group dynamics are usually more complex than the model suggests, the stages sensitize us to the ideal of a group's evolution, which can help guide our work.

ONGOING INFLUENCES

Although you and your students might not always achieve success together, you may never know how far the ripples go from the pebble you drop into the pond. You never know how much influence you may have when you meet with your students. Sometimes you may seem to fail with a student, but underneath that "failure" may be success in a different form.

For example, one literacy program dropout felt that he had failed in everything and sought solace in alcohol. But he insisted that his teenage son stay in school, that he not become a dropout like his father. The hope of learning was not strong enough to sustain the father, but the glimpse of the skills he might have had strengthened this man's concern for his son.

On the other hand, you may be teaching a potential leader. Leaders sometimes come from unlikely places. As a volunteer, you can have profound effects on the lives you touch.

In the world of finance, investment counselors use the phrase "growth potential." Consider that phrase as you tutor. It is possible that through your work and influence with a parent the attitude of a whole family could change. The children may begin to look at their parents with new respect, regarding their own learning as being more important than they had realized. With learning as a central focus for both children and parents, the whole idea of staying in school and completing an education takes on new meaning.

As you work with students from different backgrounds, you'll never know whether they or their children might become leaders or influence someone else destined for leadership. This is a growth potential with possibilities that extend far beyond your instruction.

Your constant reassurance is needed. Good tutors encourage their students to take responsibility for their own learning, letting them know that home study and practice are a real part of each session. The habits of reading and writing must be exercised every day, not only to progress but also to keep from losing these skills.

Volunteers, whether tutors or students, readers or nonreaders, need support and encouragement to get involved in other aspects of learning. Be sure that you, as a tutor, both get and give support. Look to your program and other training opportunities for continuing in-service training and support.

CONTINUING RESEARCH on best practices for teaching reading indicates that word identification skills (sometimes called "alphabetics"), phoneme awareness (identifying individual sounds with letters), decoding and sight word recognition, fluency, and vocabulary all lead to comprehension.

The goal of reading is comprehension. The above components of reading reinforce each other and are not necessarily sequential. We suggest a multi-strategy, balanced approach to reading, depending on the learning styles, ability, interest, and motivation of individual learners.

Your responsibility as a tutor/teacher is to see that individual needs are adequately addressed. Before you can teach skills to others, you must be confident that you understand those skills and can demonstrate and teach their uses. This chapter includes some effective techniques to use for developing certain skills within your teaching situation. It is important for you to be comfortable with a variety of techniques if you are to plan learner-centered lessons.

In this chapter you will be introduced to the following basic techniques for helping your students develop or extend proficiency with reading and writing, always keeping in mind that comprehension is basic to all:

- Language Experience
- sight words and context clues
- phonics
- word patterns

When you learn how to use and adapt these techniques, you will be able to incorporate them into your lessons as indicated by your assessment of students' particular needs.

A lesson will not necessarily include all of these techniques. In fact, you will recognize that many students will not need to work with some of them. Remember adult learners' need for immediate relevance as you select the most appropriate techniques for them. Also, bear in mind that the language components are integrated; therefore, it is not recommended that any lesson be spent on repeated drills of isolated components or "fragmented subskills."

As you read this chapter, recognize that some techniques are isolated for the purpose of discussion and explanation. If you feel your students would benefit from seeing how a word pattern (or some other technique) may make other words more predictable, you should address that through a prominent pattern in the material being read or written by the students. This is, of course, more relevant to the students than selecting a pattern (e.g., *-ack*) for drill on worksheets. Remember to select your teaching strategies but weigh your choices against the five themes that pervade this book. (See Introduction, page 10.)

LANGUAGE EXPERIENCE

An important element of this tutoring/teaching process is the Language Experience Approach. Language Experience is a story or experience dictated by a student and written by the tutor. Using both the learners' own experiences and language as the basis for instructional material is an effective way of collaborating with learners from the very first lesson. This approach gives immediate success and is an ice-breaker in a new teaching situation. It also gives you insights into the learners' worlds that can be of great help in selecting materials for a series of lessons.

In Language Experience, the emphasis is on demonstrating the connections between thought and oral language as written language through dictation. Language Experience can be used with those students whose experiences with writing are so severely limited or negative that they need continued demonstrations of the connections between their thoughts and written language. This technique allows even beginning readers to create sophisticated oral compositions which they can easily produce. Language Experience also works well with any level or group in which one person writes as the others talk. Eventually it can be the basis for students writing their own stories.

To see one's own words written down provides the best of all possible motivations, for it is an individual's own story. The experience story is an expression in a learner's own words of

- a personal experience;
- a dream or goal;
- a procedure from work;
- material which has been read to the learner;
- anything else of interest or concern to the learner.

Steps in Using the Language Experience Approach

1. Converse to identify an experience or topic. • Invite your students to talk. If students are hesitant or reluctant to talk, take the initiative. Read a few paragraphs from a newspaper or magazine article that you think the students will find interesting. Show a picture from a newspaper or a book and ask what is happening. Or you might ask what they enjoy doing, for leisure or for work. You'll often find that students have skills in specific areas that are much better than your skills. Perhaps one student expresses interest in woodworking or in sewing—those may not be your skills at all. That student probably can teach you something about woodworking or sewing.

Quiet and sympathetic listening will be necessary as you discover the interests and concerns of your students. Learners may need time for thoughtful reflection. Ask leading questions, but do not pressure. Give periods of silence: signs of thoughtful reflection in preparation for speaking should signal silence from you. However, extended periods of silence accompanied by signs of restlessness and embarrassment should prompt you to speak, perhaps rephrasing a question or statement that your students may not have understood.

Some groups prefer using the democratic process of voting. Ask individual students to suggest topics, limiting the choice of subjects to three, and voting to see which topic is chosen by the majority. One group chose as their three topics *gardening, soccer,* and *dancing.* Their final choice for the topic of their Language Experience was *gardening.* Together they decided on the first sentence: *We start planning for our gardens in mid winter.*

2. Record the students' words. • When working with a single student, it is simple to record the student's words. You may wish to use a sheet of carbon paper or type into a computer so that you'll have a copy for your own file. For ease of recognition, use the manuscript writing style shown in the Appendix (see page 170) as a model. Neatly print the words your student says. If the student talks faster than you can write, ask to have a sentence repeated. Your student will enjoy this. If using the computer, type the words so you and the student can see them on the screen. When teaching a beginning reader, keep the first dictated story as short as possible.

Similarly, with several students in a small group, write on the board or on paper the words the group has decided on. A leader who speaks generally for the group may emerge, but encourage participation by all.

If your students can write even in a limited way, encourage them to write at least a short Language Experience. If they are reluctant to write, offer to take dictation in these first attempts.

Do not call attention to your students' English usage in early lessons. If the dictation is *"Me and my wife…"* or *"We sure does…"* write it exactly that way. If it is simply a mispronunciation or a dialect different from standard English, such as the word *ax* for *ask,* write the word conventionally.

Later, as you work with your students, you may find that they want help with grammar and usage. That is the time to make suggested changes.

Many dialects eliminate or modify the middle and final sounds in words. For example, the word *floor* is often pronounced as if it were spelled *flo* in some language communities. In another community, natives say *"Pahk y'cah"* (Park your car), also omitting the *r* sound. It is important not to regard such modifications as incorrect. You may not realize how often you modify letter-sound relationships in the middle of words. We hear countless examples of such modifications every day. Every speaker speaks a dialect, just as every speaker speaks with an accent. Don't stress these dialectical differences, but write the words, spelling them correctly.

3. Read the story. • Make sure your students are able to see the page or the board on which you have written. Then say *"Here's what you said. Watch and listen carefully while I read it to you. Is this the way you want it written?"* Read the entire message. If you are at a computer, you can read from the screen, or print copies

for yourself and each student. Point to each word as you read. When pointing, be sure to use a pencil, ruler, or one finger as a pointer, sliding along the words. Do not point with your whole hand because the learners will not know which finger is the pointer. Say the words naturally in meaningful groups even though you are going slowly. Avoid "word calling" or saying each word separately.

Reread the first sentence, pointing to each word as you read it, sliding along to keep from reading word-by-word. Then ask the learners to read the sentence with you as you or your students slide a finger under the words. This may take a little encouragement for shy students, especially those who can't read at all. You could remind them that they already know what the sentence says because these are their own words. Feel free to tell them words they're stuck on. Read the sentence again with your students until they seem more confident. Make the reading challenging but not painful.

If learning proceeds slowly, concentrate on one sentence. If your students learn more quickly, use as much of the story as they can absorb. Reading more than one sentence at a time will help keep the meaning of the whole passage in mind. This attention to meaning helps build both comprehension and fluent reading.

4. Ask students to select meaningful words. • Help your students read some of the words from their stories out of context (that is, separate from the stories)

The following story could have been told by one student or by several:

> We got new jobs. It's packing bags at the supermarket. You got to put things in a bag just so or you'll bust them. We get tired, but we like the pay.

If your student is a beginning reader, you'll probably focus only on the first sentence. You'll want to make word cards for each word.

We	got	new	jobs

For intermediate or more advanced students, have them choose three or four meaningful words from the story that they want to learn first. Underline each of these words in the story and copy each word on a word card. Encourage students to write their own word cards as soon as possible.

jobs	supermarket	tired	pay

In the above story the words *jobs, supermarket, tired,* and *pay* might have been the meaningful words that were chosen to be learned first.

5. Teach each selected word. • Ask the students to look at each word card carefully. Say the word as written, asking the students to repeat the word. Ask the students to place each word card under its duplicate in the story, reading the word as matching takes place. Then ask the students to mix up the cards, and ask the students to read each word again, referring to the story if necessary.

Make another set of word cards for your own file, placing them in a box as a "word bank" for use in writing, spelling, and quick practicing or as a source of review. Maintaining a complete set of words learned shows your students their steady progress.

6. Reread the story. • Ask the students to reread the story (or a single sentence if you are working with low-level readers) with you. Be sure to read in meaningful phrases or sentences. You may want to ask students to reread the story on their own if you think they are ready. By rereading the story you are returning the individual words you've been working on back to their context, the story. Rereading also provides learners with the opportunity to read for meaning.

7. Give students a copy of the story and word cards. • If you have one student, give him or her the original copy of the story along with the word cards to take home for reading practice. Be sure you keep a copy for your files. If there are several students, suggest that they copy the story, or give them one of the carbon copies or copies from a copy machine or printer. You might suggest they think of other words that they want to learn from the story and make word cards for these words.

Your students can progress from dictating simple stories to being responsible for writing them later. What is important at this stage is to see their own spoken words in written form.

Examples of Student Stories

Experience stories, like the following examples, can lead to learning other skills as well.

One learner, Jonathan Lloyd, told his tutor how he drove from Syracuse, New York, to Clarksdale, Mississippi. The tutor got a map and discussed *north, south, east,* and *west.* Together they planned a variety of possible trips, with the learner giving the directions. It was fun to do, and he learned quickly. He dictated the following experience story, and the tutor wrote it in manuscript:

> I live in Syracuse. I was born in Clarksdale, Mississippi. I want to go down there by car. I go south to Pennsylvania, south and west to Cleveland, Ohio, south and west to Louisville, Kentucky, south to Memphis, Tennessee, and south to Clarksdale, Mississippi.

This led to his realizing the need to read road signs and to his next project of word cards with road signs.

Another learner, Bob Jamieson, worked as a handyman in the maintenance department of a local factory. Because his reading was at a beginning level, he knew which bottles to use only by associating colors with the materials. He is now learning to read the words on the bottles, incorporating them into his experience story. Reading in this way is a practical help on the job.

> First I use a dust mop and mop the floor. Then I use other things:
> Floor Dressing (light brown)
> Disinfectant (dark green)
> Floor Soap (pink)
> Wax (white)
> Ammonia (clear like water)

A third learner, Maxine Fielding, had legal problems. She wanted to write to a lawyer, but she had little confidence in her ability to do this because her reading and writing were at a low level. She began to solve her problem by dictating a letter to her tutor which she learned to read and later copied:

> Dear Mr. J.
>
> I'm writing this letter to inquire about your assistance. The police arrested me on a charge of burglary. I was walking down the street when I heard a noise in a store. So I went to see what was going on. When I went in I saw two young boys climbing out a window in the back of the store. I explained to the police, but they don't believe me. Can you defend me?
>
> Yours truly,
> Maxine Fielding

Step-by-Step—Language Experience

1. Identify an experience or topic through conversation.
2. Record students' words exactly as spoken.
3. Read the story, asking the students to read the story after you.
4. Ask the students to select meaningful words. Underline those words and put them on individual word cards.
5. Teach each selected word. Ask the students to shuffle the word cards and read them, referring to the story if necessary.
6. Reread the story together. Ask the students to reread the story.
7. Give a copy of the story and word cards to the students for home study, keeping a copy for yourself.

As your students progress and can read more of the words they dictate in their stories, you might want to teach only those words that they cannot read.

When you and your students have developed a text using the Language Experience Approach, you can use it as a basis for the following techniques.

SIGHT WORDS AND CONTEXT CLUES

A sight vocabulary is a stock of words immediately recognized and understood by the reader. Sight words are learned as complete units, as whole words. It is important for a reader to develop a large and growing command of such words in order to reach the major goal of reading—to understand the meaning of what is being read. Learning to recognize and identify words by sight is an essential part of any reading program.

Lists of words can be taught, but students remember them more easily if they are in meaningful groups and the students know their meanings. Experience texts or writings, whether dictated or written by the students, and printed material in the students' interest areas can provide a rich source of sight words.

Sight words are taught by having the learners look at one word at a time and associating the printed word with the spoken word. Carefully write in manuscript the words you are teaching on small cards, flashcards.

Your students probably know the meanings of most of the words because they come from their own vocabularies and from their own stories and printed materials in their interest areas.

A sight vocabulary helps readers predict what words are most likely to make sense in a given story, increases reading fluency, and leads to better comprehension.

Types of Sight Words

There are four types of words you will want to teach as sight words:

1. Survival words.
2. Service or utility words.
3. Irregularly spelled words.
4. Introductory words in word patterns (rhyming words).

Survival words are those words that students need immediately in day-to-day living. These can be related to safety, jobs, consumerism, family—whatever students need to be able to read. Safety-related survival words include *danger, police, hospital, emergency,* and *poison.* Examples of job-related survival words are *social security, company, office worker, official,* and *deduction.* Consumer-related survival words include *post office, sale, repair, bank, loan,* and *warranty.*

Service or utility words like *the, a, and, but, when, where, how,* and *why* occur frequently in written material but are often not phonetically regular. They are abstract and do not bring to mind any mental images to aid understanding.

Irregularly spelled words such as *of, have, who,* and *give* must also be taught as sight words.

Introductory words in a patterned series (see Appendix, pages 179–190) are usually taught as sight words. Thus, *make* would be taught as a sight word if it is not already known from the *-ake* pattern. *Bake* and *cake* would then be taught as patterned words.

Sight words will occur naturally in your students' Language Experience stories and other materials such as books, manuals, newspapers, notices, signs, forms, and survival word lists.

Sometimes tutors find themselves only teaching lists instead of teaching reading. Memorizing lists of unrelated words—that is, words unrelated to the topic of the lesson, to each other, or to the learners' needs—is not always helpful. The key is to use lists that are relevant to individual learners. A homemaker usually keeps a list of items needed at the store. A security officer might need a checklist while making the rounds. Many of us keep lists of things we must do: make a dental appointment, call the school, check on the telephone bill. These lists can be used as teaching tools.

However, eventually all words are read by sight and even beginning readers must have a stock of easily read words. There are lists in the Appendix of the most frequently used words (see page 191), words used in filling out forms (see page 194), and road, health, and emergency signs that students must be able to read (see pages 192–193). A worthwhile activity might be for you and your students to construct personal word lists.

Teaching Sight Words

Select, with your students, a limited number of words from the material you are reading to be taught as sight words. Six to eight new sight words per lesson are generally appropriate. You may find it necessary to select fewer for some students in the beginning as you build confidence. After working with your students for a while, you will be better able to judge how many words they can handle.

Ask your students to pick one word. Ask them to write the new sight word in manuscript on a small card. If a student is a non-writing beginner, you, the tutor, can write the word on a card. Students who can write in cursive may want to write the word in cursive on the other side of the card.

have   *have*   the   *the*

Have the students put the word into a new sentence. Either you or your students can write the new sentence in manuscript on a piece of paper. Putting the word into a context clarifies its meaning and provides clues for remembering the word.

Have your students read the word while looking at the word card and then match the word card to its mate in the sentence, saying the word as it is being matched.

Go on to the next word if the match is completed. Repeat the above until you have introduced all the sight words for that lesson. If the match is not completed, review the word and new sentence. Avoid excessive repetition as it only frustrates the students.

Ask the students to shuffle the word cards and practice rereading them, returning to the written sentences as necessary. File "known" word cards, and keep separate those that need more practice.

A general rule is that students "know" any word they can read out of context at three separate sessions. It is helpful to put a check on the back of the word card if they can read it correctly and then use it in a sentence. Three checks on a word card indicates the word is "known." As soon as your students can read a word easily over more than three lessons, that word can be put into a file box as a known word.

Similar Looking Words • Your students may sometimes confuse words that look alike (went, want). In this case, it is helpful to teach one word so thoroughly that the sight of it calls forth an immediate response. For example, have the students do the following:

1. Read the word aloud from the word card.
2. Place the word in a sentence.
3. Write the word as it is said.
4. Name the letters that compose the word.

Remove the other word that originally caused confusion and do not introduce this word until the first word has been so thoroughly learned that confusion is no longer likely. This is called *over-learning*. The second word of the pair may be introduced later without difficulty because the earlier learning is so complete that your students no longer need to consciously think about what the word is.

One of the skills that you want your students to have is the ability to recognize the same words in many contexts. But remember, beginning readers have to see a new word many times before it becomes part of their sight vocabulary. You will need to provide much practice within varied contexts to help word recognition become automatic.

Step-by-Step—Sight Words

1. You and your students select words to be taught as sight words from experience stories, reading material, students' personal lists, or students' survival word lists.

2. Ask your students to pick one word.

3. Write or have the students write the word in manuscript on a small card. (Have them write it in cursive, too, on the reverse side, if they write in cursive).

4. Ask the students to put the word in a new sentence. You or the students can write the new sentence on a piece of paper.

5. Teach the word by having the students read the word aloud while looking at the word card.

6. Have your students match the word card to the word in the sentence, saying the word as it is being matched.

7. Go on to the next word if the sequence is completed. If not, go back to Step 5.

8. Ask the students to shuffle the word cards and practice rereading them.

9. File "known word" cards. Keep others for additional practice.

Context Clues

Building a sight word (or memorized) vocabulary is a part of tutoring at all reading levels. When students recognize many words in a sentence on sight, they can often figure out the meaning of the entire sentence and thus read words in their spoken vocabulary that they would not otherwise be able to read. This ability to note what makes sense in a passage is called using context clues. The use of context clues is a skill that all good readers possess.

For example, in the sentence *"I want to l_____ more about the world,"* new readers might predict accurately that the word beginning with *l* is *learn* if they know the other words in the sentence and the sound of *l*, and if *learn* is in their speaking vocabularies.

You will want to give your students a great deal of practice in using context to predict words. This will keep your students focused on reading for meaning from the very first lessons. With very beginning readers you could use traffic signs like *STOP*, other signs like *WOMEN* or *MEN*, or items such as checks, menus, and forms to introduce the targeted sight word. The context is then the form or sign itself.

The Cloze Procedure

One way to gain proficiency in the use of context clues is to use a variation of the cloze procedure for practice. In this procedure, a person supplies words that have been deleted from a text. This technique demonstrates that people use their knowledge of the world and of language to predict as they read, that reading is a combination of many factors all operating at once.

Encourage your students to predict or guess as they read. Do not interrupt them to correct substitutions. Give time for self-correction. If that does not occur, note what kind of substitution was made and check at the end of the reading. If a word with the same meaning has been substituted, just point to the word missed and ask if the learners can read it. If a word with a completely different meaning has been substituted, ask comprehension questions about the meaning of the sentence. Supply the correct word if you sense frustration. To prepare materials for cloze exercises, any of the following techniques may be used:

1. Use materials easily read by the students. Delete words that require students to use either parts of speech or meaning clues to replace the word logically. Supply one logical replacement and another choice. Have the students read through the activity, searching for the words that make sense:

   Just as _____ have fur, birds have _____ .
       (coats, animals)   (feathers, wings)

   I go to the farmer's market to buy fresh _____ and _____ .
             (pencils, vegetables) (plants, books)

2. When learners have used the technique described above and can replace the appropriate words from the choices supplied, provide passages in which every fifth word or every tenth word is arbitrarily deleted and only a letter or two of the correct word is available, perhaps a beginning consonant or consonant blend:

   With the price of f_____ going up all the t_____ , more people are trying t_____ raise some of their f_____ in their own back y_____ .

   With the price of food going up all the time, more people are trying to raise some of their food in their own back yards.

3. When the learners do well with this task, indicate only the blank with no additional clues. Accept any word that seems a reasonable fit:

   Instead of grass, you _____ rows of lettuce, tomatoes, _____ beans lining the fences _____ in the biggest city.

   Instead of grass, you find rows of lettuce, tomatoes, and beans lining the fences even in the biggest city.

Many computer programs teach sight words through cloze activities.

PHONICS: LETTER-SOUND RELATIONSHIPS

It's important for our students to be aware of phonemes, and to be able to detect these individual sounds of letters or groups of letters within words. Phonics, a way of teaching reading that makes use of phonetic values of letters, letter groups, and syllables, helps students see and hear this connection between letters and the sounds they represent.

Phonics is the one technique which takes longer to demonstrate in a text than to teach. Most adults know the names of the letters, but phonics helps students discover the connections between *letters* and *sounds*. Many students may already know these connections. Through your early assessment (see Chapter 8 on Assessment), if you find that your students know all the letter-sound correspondences, then there is no need for phonics instruction. However, if you find a student has trouble with a few or all specific letter-sound combinations, you can use this technique.

As a base for understanding phonics instruction, it is useful to know that we use thousands of words in talking, reading, and writing, but only 26 letters are used to spell these words. These 26 letters are called the *alphabet.* They represent 42-44 sounds. Most of the letters in the alphabet are called *consonants*. Five of the letters—*a, e, i, o, u*—are called *vowels*. Sometimes *y* is used as a vowel.

Point to a letter in a word and explain to your students that each letter is a symbol. Explain that words are made up of groups of letters. Point to an entire sentence and explain that a sentence is made up of a group of words. Note that the first word of a sentence begins with a capital letter and that most sentences end with a period.

Because people learn in different ways that are not always predictable or completely understood, successful reading and writing instruction can often be accomplished best by using several approaches at the same time. Some people seem to learn words as a whole. Many words in English can be learned this way because they do not break down readily into sound units. Other words can be recognized through the analysis of letters and letter clusters. Every word in English contains at least some sound-symbol clues to help the reader.

There are many ways to teach letter-sound relationships. Any way is acceptable if it works with your students. The important thing is that your students associate sounds with letters and groups of letters. After learning a basic technique, you may find other creative ideas for teaching letter-sound relationships. Adapt the system to meet each student's needs.

Many students are not aware of the complexity of sounds that make up a spoken word. Students vary in their ability to perceive sounds. This may be evidence of a hearing problem. Since many of these problems are correctable and will affect learning to read, students may find it useful to get hearing tests if at all possible.

Remember, too, that some people can hear very well but cannot distinguish one sound from another in speech and/or hearing. They may lack auditory discrimination of one sound or perhaps several sounds. If that is the situation, they may have a good deal of trouble with phonics instruction. You will probably need to tread lightly, being careful not to frustrate students. Use other strategies.

To decide if auditory discrimination may be the problem, take two words that sound exactly alike except for one sound (for example, *set* and *sit* or *mat* and *met* or *pot* and *put;* for native speakers of the English language, vowels are usually the tricky ones). If you find that your students cannot distinguish your pronunciation of *sit* from *set,* you may have students with auditory discrimination problems. You will only frustrate them if you try to get them to read or write based on a sound distinction that they may never have heard or spoken.

In fact, different dialect communities vary pronunciation and do not themselves differentiate in the pronunciation of certain sounds. For example, some communities say *witch* and *which* the same way. Others pronounce *pen* and *pin* the same. Still others equate *Yale* and *yell.* Being aware of differences in pronunciation and complications from problems with auditory discrimination can help you be sensitive to students who do not respond well to phonics instruction. Above all, if students pronounce a word differently from the way you do, do not tell them they are wrong; they are not. Their sound system is just different from yours.

You cannot teach your students to use letter-sound relationships unless you know them yourself. If you are unsure of the sounds, review them aloud, listening carefully as you pronounce the words related to each letter as suggested in the Appendix, Suggested Key Words—Phonics (see page 178).

If students are complete nonreaders, you may want to teach only one letter per lesson. Remember, you'll be introducing experience stories, sight words, and patterned words, too. If phonics work is needed, be sure to keep the phonics part of each lesson short and related to the material being used. Phonic exercises may be tiring to your students. Tell your students why phonics is an important part of the lesson. Recognizing the sounds that letters represent will help students identify new words.

Only paper and a pen or pencil—no specific books—are needed for teaching phonics. You will want to look at the list of Suggested Key Words (see page 178). You can supplement this list with words from your students' experience writings as well as from newspapers, magazines, and available books—words to which the students can relate.

These exercises are meant for those who need help in learning all letter names and sounds. Don't re-teach phonic skills if your students already recognize letters and their corresponding sounds. But if you find students who consistently miscall the sound of a specific letter, perhaps mixing *d* and *b,* or not knowing the sound for *k* or *w,* use this technique to assist them. If you find that letter-sound instruction frustrates or confuses students, emphasize some other techniques. Before attempting to teach, carefully study the instructions provided.

Begin by teaching the letters that each student needs—those identified in the student's assessment. Some phonics materials start teaching letter-sound combinations alphabetically. Because the sound of *b* and some of the early consonants are more difficult to pronounce, we suggest teaching those letters that have sustained sounds, */m/, /s/, /f/,* first because they are easier to say and hear.

In the teaching examples that follow, letter names are shown as *s, f;* letter sounds are shown as */s/, /f/.*

Consonants

You and your students will be creating a letter-sound dictionary as you proceed with the instructions that follow. Provide one sheet of paper or a 3" x 5" card for each letter, using the following format for teaching consonants.

Action	Tutor Says	Student's Response
Tutor writes *s* in manuscript and points to it. s	This is an *s.*	
	What is the name of this letter?	*s*
	Listen for the sound of *s* at the beginning of these words— *sun, sink, socks, sandwich.* Do you hear the sound?	yes
	Say these words after me while listening for the beginning sound: *sun* *sink* *socks* *sandwich*	*sun* *sink* *socks* *sandwich*

| | Which of these *s* words—*sun, sink, socks, sandwich*—do you want for your key word to help you remember the sound of *s*? | (Student selects word. Let's assume the word *sun* is selected.) |

(A key word will always mean more if the student can identify with it. Words beginning with blends such as *snake* or *tree* should not be used as key words. It is easier for students to use words with single beginning consonants. You might suggest a key word from an experience story. You should make sure that key words are words students can "see." For example, *best* is not a good key word because it does not evoke a mental picture. Better key words would be *bus, baby,* or *bed* because students can visualize these objects.)

Action	Tutor Says	Student's Response
Tutor writes student's key word in manuscript under *s*. s sun	*Sun* is your key word to help you remember the sound of *s*.	
	Think of the beginning sound in *sun*. Now, let out just the first sound. (In the beginning you may need to say, "Notice how you hold your lips, tongue, and teeth.")	/s/

(If the student fails to make the desired response within a reasonable time, you might supply it: /s/ is the sound of the letter s.)

	Here are some words. Listen. Do these words start with the *s* sound?	
	sausage	yes
	forest	no
	Monday	no
	salad	yes
	summer	yes
	Now, let's move this sound to the end of the word. Listen to the last sound in these words, and repeat the words:	
	gas	*gas*
	kiss	*kiss*
	boss	*boss*
	What is the last sound in these words?	/s/
Tutor points to *s*.	What is the name of this letter?	s

s

sun

Tutor points to *sun*.	What is your key word?	*sun*
	What is the sound of *s*?	/s/
Student writes as tutor points.	Will you write an *s* right here?	

s   s

sun

(A beginning student may need more writing practice with individual letters, using your manuscript letters as models.)

Tutor prints capital *S*.

s S   s S

sun

This is a capital *S*, the same name, the same sound. You use a capital letter for a name that begins with *S* or the first word in a sentence.

(If your student already writes in cursive, you and the student should write the *s* and *S* in cursive, too.)

(More written words can be added to the *s* page later.)

s S   s S

sun

sink

sandwich

If your students learn quickly and if phonics is a review, it is not necessary to have a separate page for each letter. You might want to put all the letters and individual words on one sheet for home study. You may prefer to use 3" x 5" cards instead of sheets of paper. Use one card for each letter, having the students write the letter and the key word on them. Cards are convenient for review.

Use the preceding format to practice the instructional procedures for the consonants. You should be thoroughly familiar with the instructional procedure before you begin teaching your students.

This practice may seem excessive, but experience has shown that thorough familiarity with these procedures is essential to your success with this technique.

Letter-Sound Activities

Some students have problems distinguishing individual sounds in words. If, after reasonable instruction, you fail to note any progress in relating sounds to letters, instruct by reading to your students, having them follow along using the sight word technique. You might want to try again a little later on to see if they can learn letter-sound associations.

When working on letters and sounds with students who can read only a very limited number of words, give them something to do that looks like reading.

Using a newspaper, have the students look for the known letters (perhaps circling them) and review the names of the letters, key words, and sounds. This is an effective way of using the newspaper at the level of even a beginning student's ability.

Your students could also spell the beginning and ending letters of a word. Point to objects around the room, such as the door, a book, some paper, a pen, and ask your students to name the objects and then identify the beginning and ending sounds. Use only items that incorporate known sounds.

Step-by-Step—Phonics (Consonants)

1. Tutor names the letter. Tutor writes it. Student repeats the letter name.
2. Student listens for the sound of the letter at the beginning of some words while the tutor says the words and then while the student says them.
3. Student picks a key word. Tutor writes the word.
4. Student produces the sound of the letter by producing the beginning sound of the key word.
5. Student listens and recognizes the sound in the beginning of other words.
6. Student listens and recognizes the sound at the end of words.
7. Student produces the sound at the end of words.
8. Student and tutor review the name, sound, and key word for the letter.
9. Student writes the letter.
10. Tutor explains and writes the capital letter.

Consonant Blends

If your student has learned words that begin or end with single consonants, it is now possible to teach blends without requiring any new knowledge. Blends are two consonants in a row with the two sounds blending together (*bl, cr*). Merely blend in the additional consonant with the word the student already knows. For example, if the learner knows *lag* as a word, the addition of the consonant *f* (representing the sound /*f*/) will yield *flag*. *Top* becomes *stop* by the simple addition of one letter sound. *Ben* becomes *bent* or *bend* when the sound of either *t* or *d* is added at the end. The most frequently occurring blends have *r* or *l* in the second position (*tr, cl*).

Consonant Digraphs

When teaching the digraphs (two letters with only one sound, *sh, ch, th, wh,* and *qu*), follow the same format used in teaching single consonants. Note that the sound for *th* in words like *thumb* is slightly different from its sound in words like *the*. The *th* in *thumb* is voiceless and the *th* in *the* is voiced. It is not important to stress this distinction.

Phonic Rules

English is not a phonetically regular language, but it is a patterned language. Many of the rules formerly incorporated into phonics programs have so many exceptions that they may be more confusing than enlightening to many students. For example, the rule that two vowels together usually represent the long sound of the first vowel (words such as *meat, die, dough*) is accurate for words in beginning reading books only 45 percent of the time. For words from a dictionary, this rule applies only 18 percent of the time. Consider words such as *great, threat, relieve, heard,* and *sieve.* The rule that adding an *e* at the end of a *C-V-C* word makes the vowel long is more often correct (*hat – hate; pan – pane; bit – bite*), but there are exceptions (*give, have*) that must be taught as sight words.

However, there are a few spelling rules that can be helpful.

1. The *i-e* or the *e-i* vowel combination
   I before *e* except after *c*, or when sounding like *a* as in *neighbor* or *weigh.*
2. The doubling rule
   When adding an ending (*-ing, -ed*) double the final consonant if it is preceded by a single vowel (*drop, dropping – stop, stopped*).
3. Root word with a final *e*
   In a word with a final *e*, drop the *e* before adding a suffix that begins with a vowel (*hope, hoping, hoped*).

Many reading systems teach rules for dividing words into syllables with appropriate accenting. The usefulness of such rules is questionable, since the application of the rule often requires that students already be able to pronounce the word. Consider the final syllable in words like *sudden, leader* and *system;* compare the sounds of these syllables with the consonant sounds you have just learned. In the second syllable, the vowel sound is suppressed and the consonant predominates in normal speech patterns.

It is also untrue that each vowel in a word provides its own vowel sound (*rain, made*). Therefore, if students look at a word in an effort to be able to pronounce it, they may have great difficulty in deciding which cluster of letters constitutes a syllable. This process can become so complicated that students who could follow such directions would certainly be capable of learning the word anyway.

WORD PATTERNS

Vowels

Vowels pose a major challenge in learning to read because they represent so many sounds. Frequently the sound the vowel represents can only be determined by noting the letters that follow it. Note the many ways the letter *a* can sound in various patterns.

man	*mar*	*mean*	*make*	*maw*

It is interesting to see how difficult it is to supply the correct consonant sound to complete the pattern when all you have are vowels. For example try to read this sentence:

E__e__ __i__ a____ ___e_ _o_e____ __e____ ou__,
__ou __i____ __o_i_e ___a__ __ou __a__ __ea__
____i__ __e____e__ e __ui_e ea__i___.

By contrast, try to read this sentence:

__v__n w__th __ll th__ v__w__ls l__ft ____t, y____ w__ll
n__t__c__ th__t y____ c__n r____d th__s s__nt__nc__
q____t__ ____s__ly.

Yes, when you have the consonants, the passage is very easy to read.

Even with all the vowels left out, you will notice that you can read this sentence quite easily.

Words in Pattern

Learning words by seeing word patterns enables the students to notice more readily the relationships between clusters of letters and the sounds they represent. The most prevalent letter cluster in English is the consonant-vowel-consonant (C-V-C). Here are samples of two word families of patterns:

get	*cap*
set	*map*
let	*sap*
met	*tap*

Parts of words that sound alike are often spelled alike.

Rhyming

Before you begin instruction in word patterns, it is helpful to know whether your students understand rhyming. Some adult nonreaders have not been exposed to nursery rhymes as children and may not understand that *cat* and *rat* rhyme. Such students may not even know what the word *rhyme* means. When a word rhymes with another, it agrees with that word in the ending sounds.

If your students cannot rhyme words, this technique might help. Provide your students with several rhyming words of more than one syllable, then a beginning sound to which the rhyming ending will be attached. For example, say:

"I am going to give you three rhyming words. Then I'll start the fourth word and you finish it like the rest. Listen:

colder
bolder
holder
/f/

The students should reply *"folder."* If not, supply the word and repeat the series. Then give another example, such as:

jacket
packet
/r/

Supply again, if necessary, *"racket."* Continue to give such models until the students understand rhyming. The reason for using longer words is that the students are given a greater number of common elements to help in understanding the notion of rhyming.

Once you are sure of the students' ability to rhyme, you can move to shorter clusters:

ran
man
can
/f/

with assurance that students hear the common sound and also see the letters that represent these identical clusters of sounds. Often this is a simple task, but for some students it's a challenge.

Teaching Words in Pattern

Choose a patterned word from the words your students already know. Use a simple consonant-vowel-consonant (C-V-C) word first. You will take this known word and analyze it into its beginning letter and the *C-V-C* pattern you want to teach. Remind your students what the word is. This first word is the clue from which they will figure out the rest of the words in that pattern. Always list the words vertically so that the common visual characteristics are noticed by the students.

Teach vowels as part of ending clusters because the sound that a vowel represents is usually signaled by the pattern in which it is found. Therefore, if your students learn a sound cluster—such as *-an*—as a unit, it will be more helpful than to sound out words by pronouncing each sound individually.

The basic approach to teaching word patterns involves blending the consonants with a letter grouping called a phonogram (*-at, -eg, -ick, -end*). About 100 of these phonograms combined with consonants will provide students with many words—enough to indicate the general meaning of a passage. The context clues in addition to consonants will allow the students to infer most other words. These word patterns or phonograms may be taught in the following way:

Action	Tutor says	Student's Response
Tutor writes *cap.* cap	This word is *cap.* What is this word?	 *cap*
Tutor writes *map* directly under *cap.* cap map	If *c-a-p* is *cap,* what is *m-a-p?* (If there is no answer or an incorrect answer, supply *map.*)	*map*
Tutor writes *lap.* cap map lap	And what is *l-a-p?*	*lap*
Tutor writes *sap.* cap map lap sap	And what is *s-a-p?*	*sap*
	Please reread the whole list.	*cap* *map* *lap* *sap*
	What is the same in each word?	The *–ap*
	What changes?	The first letter

(Accept the sounds of the pattern or the names of the letters.)

If your students are struggling to understand this new concept, use only three or four words in a pattern. Too many words may be confusing. More words can be added later.

For more advanced students, use more difficult words from experience stories, workbooks, or any other reading material being used. For the students who understand this concept, the possibilities are unlimited. Many words can be learned, such as:

sing	*sight*
ring	*right*
bring	*might*
spring	*bright*
string	*blight*

The technique of teaching patterned words may seem deceptively simple. Students may need to expend considerable effort until they see that words having common letter clusters often have common sound clusters. It is worthwhile to continue to use this technique even when it does not bring immediate success. Its power is immense when students catch on.

There are, however, some students who do not seem to be able to learn an entire letter grouping as one unit. For these students, sounding out separate letters may be a necessary first step. This individual letter-sounding should be abandoned as soon as possible.

If, for example, your student, in reading the word *got,* says *get:*

1. Ask the student to name the letters.
2. If this does not produce *got,* say, "You gave me *g-e-t.* The word is spelled *g-o-t.*" Emphasize the letter in question.
3. If the student still does not read *got,* write *not* and ask the student to read it. Then write *got* below it, soliciting a response.
4. If the student still does not pronounce the word, you supply it.
5. Add patterned words in a column to help produce the generalization of the pattern, such as:

not
got
hot
pot
dot
cot

As your students progress, the initial consonant substitution is not always necessary because you want instant recognition of larger letter clusters. The goal is to have your students recognize the entire letter cluster, such as *man* in *manage* or *sat* in *satisfy.* Such clusters provide the structure for words with more than one syllable. Learning many such clusters establishes the basis for independent word attack.

This method emphasizes the vowel as part of the word pattern rather than in isolation. Most students will find learning vowels in patterns less confusing than trying to remember distinctions between long vowels, short vowels, vowels affected by *r, l, w,* etc.

Lists of patterned words are in the Appendix (see pages 179–190).

Long Vowel Sounds in Pattern • It is easy to identify a long vowel sound in spoken words because the sound is the same as the letter name. It is often more difficult to identify the long vowel sounds in written words because in English the sound is represented by so many different letter clusters. For example, the long vowel *o* might be spelled as follows:

o as in *so*
oa as in *coat*
oe as in *toe*
ow as in *blow*
ough as in *dough*
eau as in *beau*

Teach clusters of words giving the long vowel sound by using the word pattern procedure. (See Appendix pages 179–190.) You would teach:

coat
boat
goat

in one long *o* pattern and

toe
foe
hoe

at another session.

In addition, clusters that look alike often result in different sounds. For example:

Ew as in *sew* is different from *ew* in *blew*.
Ow in *now* is different from *ow* in *show*.
Ou as in *found* is different from *ou* in *group, young, four, though* or *thought*.

It is usually easier to teach one of the sound patterns (*cow, now, how*) before teaching the other pattern (*low, slow, blow*).

Once your students understand the concept of rhyming, word patterns are easy to teach and fun to work with. Enjoy this technique and use it often.

In reading a passage, if your students come across unknown words with spellings that can have more than one sound, suggest that they try both sounds and select the word that makes sense in that sentence. Or, if your student sees a word in a text that he can't read, you might suggest that he ask himself these questions:

1. What is the sound of the first letter?
2. Are there any patterns I know within this word?
3. Are there any context clues that will help me with this word?

You're giving your students various skills to help them read independently.

Step-by-Step—Word Patterns

1. Tutor writes the first word in a pattern, saying the letters and the word.

2. Tutor writes the second pattern word directly under the first, using a beginning sound the students know. Tutor asks the students to read the word.

3. If the students respond correctly, the tutor adds more words in pattern asking the students to read the words.
   If the students give no response or a wrong response, the tutor reviews possible elements of difficulty:
   a. The students may not remember the beginning sound.
   b. The students may not remember the sound of the letter cluster.

4. Tutor asks the students to read the list of patterned words.

5. Tutor asks the students to identify the letters that are the same in all the words. Tutor accepts the sounds of the pattern or the names of the letters.

6. Tutor and students make word cards for the words in each pattern.

Multi-Syllabic Word Patterns • As your students are learning to recognize patterns, looking for patterns in words of more than one syllable within the reading materials can be helpful. By pronouncing identified patterns within longer words, students will be able to handle these words more easily. They can check their pronunciation of the word against their knowledge of what word would make sense in that context. For example, the word *passenger* is composed of three already familiar patterns:

pas/sen/ger

If the students should happen to look at the word in a slightly different way, dividing it as

pass/en/ger

it will still result in a similar pronunciation.

These word divisions may not be the traditional syllables you find in a dictionary, but it is not necessary to divide words precisely as the dictionary does in order to use this skill in multi-syllabic words. Indeed, dictionaries do not always agree on how a given word should be broken down. It is essential for your students to be able to handle the groups of letters that comprise the word.

Using the following steps, try out this skill on words such as *transportation, merchandise, combination.*

1. Students look at the word to determine what familiar patterns it contains.

2. Students indicate the clusters by marking words with a pencil:
   trans/por/ta/tion or *tran/spor/ta/tion.*

3. Tutor asks the students to pronounce each letter cluster as quickly as possible, blending them into the word. Any pronounceable combination is acceptable. If there is a slight mispronunciation, the students should recognize the word if it is known in oral language.

4. Tutor encourages the students to use the meaning clues in order to get a correct pronunciation.

5. If the students cannot do this easily, the tutor divides one or two words as examples.

buf/fa/lo

en/vel/ope

The important thing is to have your students look for recognizable letter clusters. Start with whatever part of the word your students know. Suggest that they first look for a part of the word that is familiar. Often they recognize the first syllable; sometimes they recognize the one in the middle, as in the word *struggle*. They may recognize

rug

then

trug

strug/gle

Not all words divide easily to produce a near approximation in sound to the word in question. It is just as logical to divide *apron* as *ap/ron* or *a/pron*, *business* as *bus/in/ess* or *bus/i/ness*, or *razor* as *raz/or* or *ra/zor*, but a search for meaning usually brings forth the desired recognition of the word.

Application of the skills you have taught and the clues that come from the context itself should allow the students to pronounce the word correctly. It is helpful to start with compound words that are easy to divide (ones that consist of two complete words such as *hallway, upstairs*), or with words having prefixes or suffixes (such as *compound, reflex* or *action, teller*).

Step-by-Step—Multi-Syllabic Words

1. Students look at the word, searching for familiar patterns (*outstanding*).

2. Students indicate letter clusters by slash marks (*out/stand/ing*).

3. Students pronounce each letter cluster, quickly blending into a word.

4. Students check against the context clues, asking "Does this make sense here?"

AS STUDENTS ADVANCE

These same reading and writing techniques can be adapted as students advance and for classroom use too. In this context, an advancing student is one who can write but has poor spelling, grammar, and punctuation skills, and has little self confidence. You are encouraging that student to actually write words that he or she knows and to have the courage to put words on paper as they might sound.

What about Language Experience? Ask questions to encourage students to think of their own interests and concerns, giving them opportunities to express their thoughts. Instead of the tutor writing down these first sentences, ask the students to write them down. You might get some hesitation, but repeat each sentence and add "Write it down—it's your own words."

Saying the words out loud makes the students focus on specific words and usually gives them the confidence to write because they have exact words to write. Tell them to forget about spelling, punctuation, and grammar.

An example:

Teacher: What are your special interests, your hobbies? What would you do if you had unlimited time and money?

Student: Gardening is my hobby. I like to see things grow.

Teacher: I know little of gardening. You're the expert there. You said "Gardening is my hobby." Write that down.

Student: I can't spell those words.

Teacher: What does gardening begin with? Then just put a line.

Student: g-a-r—OK, I think I can spell it.

gardening is my hobe.

Teacher: Great. And you said "I like to see things grow."

Student: I'll try it.

I like to see things gro.

Spelling, punctuation, and grammar problems can be addressed later, but the ice has been broken. Your student has actually written down his own thoughts. If the student wants it corrected, do so—otherwise type it up as is, and when corrections are made later, retype it. This is the start of your student's own book—he is now an author.

Language Experience can be just as effective when working in a small group or a classroom setting as students advance. Ask your students, individually, to suggest three subjects. Jot those three topics on the board. They could be as diverse as *soccer, voting,* or *our jobs.* Remind your students that we live in a democracy—one person/one vote—and that each student has a vote. Take the vote, noting that the non-winning topics can be the basis for future discussions.

Let's say *"our jobs"* wins. Challenge the students to discussion, perhaps asking questions: *"Where do you work?" "What do you do?" "Why are your jobs important?" "What are your concerns?"* Ask for a volunteer to write what the students say. They might come up with something like this:

We need better jobs to take care of our families. How can we get better jobs?

You can stop here and have the students read and copy the story, putting words that are troubling on cards for more study. Then more discussion and more of their own story. This can be the beginning of a group project where the stronger students can help those who need more help.

What about phonics? If your advancing students understand the relationship of sound to symbol of all the consonants, there are no problems with phonics. However, if there are a few unknown letter sounds, teach them as taught in this chapter. They're probably ready for blending letter sounds (*bl, cr, br,* etc.), and for working on prefixes (*pre-, dis-,* etc.) and suffixes (*-tion, -ing,* etc.)

You'll continue to teach sight words and patterned words as new and more complex words are learned, assuming that you, the tutor, have mastered those skills. You might want to work on words that are needed to fill out applications or those special words seen daily on signs (see Appendix, pages 192–194).

SUMMARY

Reading and writing fluency is blocked in most beginning students by their inability to recognize printed words quickly and accurately. You now have a number of approaches to help your students learn to do this.

Skills	Sources	Goals
Reading/Writing using	Experience stories	Reading/Writing with fluency and comprehension
Sight words	Real life materials	
Phonics	Newspapers	
Word patterns	Magazines	
Critical thinking	Work-related materials	
	Books, basic texts	
	Word lists	
	Workbooks	
	Anything of interest to students	

Throughout your teaching, check that your students understand what they're reading and writing. Without comprehension, they are not truly reading.

All of this will probably take much time. There will be high peaks of sudden discovery and long plateaus where progress may not be so dramatic. As you teach, go back to your notes on students and to early assessments. You'll probably find more progress than you would have believed possible.

If you find that some of your students have difficulties with the suggested techniques, slow down and focus on smaller "chunks." There are additional suggestions in Chapter 10—Learning Disabilities and Learning Differences.

TEACHING READING—COMPREHENSION, FLUENCY, VOCABULARY

Introducing Reading Strategies
Before Reading
During Reading
After Reading

Comprehension
Literal Interpretation
Inference
Critical Thinking
Example—Buying a Car
Retention

Fluency in Reading
Modeled Reading
Silent Reading Following a Leader
Choral Reading
Impress or Shadow Reading
Phrase Reading

Vocabulary

Summary

STUDENTS CAN GAIN CONFIDENCE and practice in building meaning during their reading if they are aware of and consciously try to do what many good readers do when they read. Proficient readers instinctively have a kind of dialogue with a text before, during, and after reading.

Before reading, good readers usually examine the text, make predictions about the nature of the reading, flip through the pages to see the format and the illustrations, and make sure it looks like something they'd like to read.

During reading, good readers often talk to themselves, making sure they understand what they've been reading, summarizing key ideas if they're reading difficult material, rereading if they find they're not understanding. They also check to see if their predictions were accurate; and update those predictions as they read further along in the text. This "self-talk" can be silent or aloud, but either way it allows readers the opportunity to check their understanding.

Sometimes good readers take notes; sometimes they go to the dictionary. They often quickly skim non-technical material. Proficient readers vary the strategies they use when they read depending on the difficulty of the text and their interest in and knowledge about the subject.

After reading, good readers usually "respond" to the material. After reading fiction, poetry, or inspirational essays, readers often respond emotionally: "I loved the ending." "I can't believe it ended that way." "Margaret was such an admirable character." "I wish the story was not over." After the emotional response good readers are ready to look at other aspects of the text: "What did I learn?" "Did I guess right?" "Did any of my predictions prove true?" "How does it compare with something else I've read or with my experience?" "What were the new words?"

INTRODUCING READING STRATEGIES

Readers are generally not aware of the strategies they use. You can work to help new readers understand why strategies are important and help them incorporate this kind of self-talk into their own reading. Below are guidelines to help you translate these strategies to your students as you tutor.

Before Reading:

1. **Get students into the habit of previewing and predicting.** Suggest that your students look at the title, chapter headings, subheadings, bold type, and illustrations before reading the text. Through these activities, they are making connections in their minds between the subject of the material and what they already know. You might want to ask them to predict what they think the passage will be about. Remember, you are working with adults and need to recognize the rich background knowledge and experience many bring to a reading passage.

2. **If the material has a summary, have students read it first and retell it to you in their own words.** If students cannot paraphrase (retell the story or

text in their own words), suggest that you or the students read the summary one more time and try again. If students still cannot paraphrase, you do the paraphrasing as a model and proceed.

3. **Help students to identify the type of text.** Is it a poem, an essay, a story, a technical manual, a job application form? Knowing the type of text will help students make predictions and identify purposes for reading.

4. **Help students identify the purpose for reading.** Are they reading for pleasure, for information, for instruction, to pass a test, to be inspired? Their purpose for reading will impact the strategies they choose to use during reading.

During Reading:

1. **Encourage students to check constantly for meaning.** They need to be asking themselves, "Does this make sense?" Your purpose here is to encourage active reading, a kind of dialogue between readers and the text. This is the time to check predictions and make new ones.

2. **During silent reading, when students come to a word they don't know, suggest that they skip the word and read on.** Usually the meaning will come through the context.

3. **When they are reading aloud, if students come to words they stumble over, supply the words quietly and allow them to read on.**

4. **In oral reading, help students read in phrases rather than word-by-word.** You may need to model this procedure. There's more on phrase reading later in this chapter.

After Reading:

1. **Allow for the emotional response if it's appropriate to the type of reading you've been doing.** You can do this easily by asking, "What did you think about . . . ?"

2. **Do a quick comprehension check, based on the kind of text.**

   a. **Ask students to summarize the reading by talking or writing.** If the reading material describes a process the students need to repeat, ask the students to describe the process step-by-step.

   b. **If the reading is an opinion piece, ask the students to restate the writer's opinion and then to agree or disagree with the opinions expressed in the reading.** Your main questions will be "What is the author's view?" and "Do you agree with the author? Why or why not?"

   c. **If students want to master the material for a test, ask them to recall what they need to remember.** You or the students can make notes or lists to keep for review or future reference.

3. **If students like to keep records of new words they are learning, ask them to recall or look back to find new words from the lesson.**

Helping students learn to use strategies before, while, and after they read will improve their comprehension because it makes them aware of the active nature of the reading process.

COMPREHENSION

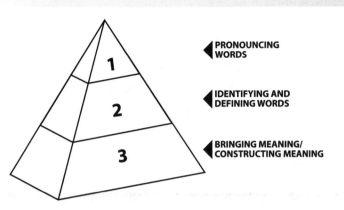

In the Three Views of Reading pyramid, comprehension or construction of personal meaning is the base. Comprehension is the accurate understanding of what is read. As you work with students, the emphasis of each lesson should be to make sense of what is read. To help attain that goal, you can introduce other strategies. However, these strategies should be seen as stepping stones to the primary goal of making sense of the text. You probably noted that comprehension is a goal in teaching all techniques of reading, including Language Experience, sight words, context clues, and word patterns.

Literal Interpretation

The literal meaning of a passage is the meaning of the words on the page. Literal interpretation does not include students' feelings or opinions. An easy check for literal meaning is to ask students to retell in their own words what they read. If this is difficult for them, you could ask such questions as "What was the story about?" or "What happened at the end?"

If students cannot retell the story, you will want to know whether the problem is one of trying to process too much material or if there is some skill lacking that prevents retelling. To see if the problem is too much material, reduce the quantity by having them read just one paragraph. If they cannot retell what the paragraph is about, deal with a single sentence or two. If this is still not successful, break the sentence into phrases by putting slash marks in pencil after words that should be read together:

Every payday / we save some money / and we put it / in the bank.

Now paraphrase this sentence for the students, modeling how to retell. Then use another sentence, suggesting that the students do the retelling.

This practice will provide a basis for literal comprehension of the author's words. Literal comprehension can occur only if the readers' personal experiences are varied enough to encompass similar ideas.

For some readers, the ideas and concepts, not the words, are out of the realm of their understanding or experience. If you find such a situation with your students, work on vocabulary to extend experience by providing pictures, explanations, or demonstrations.

Inference

When you are sure the students understand the facts the author has presented, you can ask for responses requiring higher level comprehension skills. From the stated information, you can ask students to make inferences (i.e., draw logical conclusions) about ideas not fully expressed or developed in the text.

For example, suppose students read this sentence:

As soon as Congress adjourns, senators leave Washington behind and head for home.

They might conclude that Washington is not the senators' home and perhaps is not their favorite place.

Consider this sentence:

He froze in his tracks as he heard the squeak again from the dark corner.

You could ask the students what the expression "to freeze in his tracks" means. Did he literally turn to ice? You will want the students to realize that the expression refers to emotion, not to temperature, and that tracks have something to do with stopping his motion, not with trains or jogging.

Our language is metaphorical. Our words have multiple levels of meaning. In addition, various communities have their own expressions that are not understandable to other communities.

Another simple way to introduce the multiple levels of meaning in a passage is to use proverbs, fables, or parables. Having read Aesop's fable about a fox, you could discuss the literal meaning ("There was a fox. . .") and then the various interpretive meanings ("What lesson do you think Aesop was trying to teach us?").

How do we all acquire the knowledge to be able to make inferences? It comes from a vast reservoir of information collected over a lifetime. There is no specified way to assure this information base. However, the more we read, listen, and experience, the more we encounter a rich variety of words and expressions, and the greater is our capacity to understand the next idea that comes along.

From the oral language base, we proceed to recognize words in print that represent ideas or meaning. From these perceived meanings and our own inner storehouses of information, we think beyond the words of the text in response to our own experiences. We check out the validity of such thoughts by determining whether they are consistent with what we already know. Then we feel justified in arriving at certain conclusions. When we receive, understand, and interpret the initial data from print sources, we call it reading.

Critical Thinking

Often people who have grown to adulthood without being able to read have such a reverence for the printed page that they accept everything in print as the absolute truth. Let's help students to question the authority of authors when they read materials open to interpretation (e.g., newspapers, self-help books, opinion articles), to think critically, to reason and evaluate as they read.

What is critical thinking? It is challenging assumptions, asking essential questions, reading for a purpose, analyzing as you question.

A first step is to show students the difference between facts and opinions. Good news reporting should present the facts, but the editorial page is a collection of opinions. Advice columnists give their own opinions about people's problems. Give students practice in raising questions when opinions are stated:

"What evidence does this writer give us? How does he know?"
"Does the evidence relate to the question or does it seem off the subject?"
"How did the writer collect his evidence? Who exactly does he say
he interviewed?"
"Is he an expert? What do other experts say?"
"How can we check this for ourselves?"

Reading opens doorways to thinking. Encourage your students to think of the *who, what, when, where, why,* and *how* when they are reading and writing. You can help learners clarify their thoughts through questioning:

1. Use questions to encourage discussion about events, opinions, and procedures in the reading material:

   Who would you say is the most important character? Why?

2. Ask questions that will structure students' answers in concise and logical order:

   Yes, I agree that the main character seemed to overreact to his partner. But what happened first?

3. Ask questions that will lead students to speculate or read between the lines:

   Why did so few supplies reach the people who needed them? What do you think the author wants us to think about that government?

4. Try to avoid questions that require only a yes/no response:

   What did you think about this book?

   rather than

   Did you like this book?

5. Ask students to formulate questions. This may be difficult for them at first, but after you've modeled some questions, they'll probably follow your lead. Encourage students to ask themselves these questions as they read.

- **Health issues – What about tobacco advertising? What should they believe, and what is propaganda?**
- **Voting issues – Do you take all the statements of candidates as absolute truths, or are they trying to get your vote by deception?**
- **Shopping issues – How should you look at advertising? As describing the articles involved truthfully, or are they describing the advantages but avoiding writing about negative things?**

It is harder to get students to think for themselves than to give them quick answers.

Critical thinking is important not only in things we read or what we see on TV, but in real life situations. Critical thinking should be a life-long skill.

Problems generally don't have one simple correct answer. Usually there are alternative solutions, but one must learn how to assess the best answers by thinking critically. Once your students are comfortable questioning things they read and what they see on TV or in ads, they can extend that "critical thinking" to their own personal lives, knowing that they often have choices in decision making.

Example—Buying a Car

One student was thinking of purchasing a car. But he was confused and torn because he realized how little he knew about this first time purchase. He had heard on TV that there was no need for a down payment, and he felt able to pay their described monthly payment, but he wanted help in how to think this through, as well as help in reading any documents he'd have to sign.

He and his tutor set up questions to help him "think critically and logically" before making the final decision.

After much discussion, they agreed that to show his choices he should set up six columns on a sheet of paper: (1) Advantages of purchasing a NEW car, (2) Disadvantages of purchasing a NEW car, (3) Advantages of purchasing a USED car, (4) Disadvantages of purchasing a USED car, (5) Advantages of NOT purchasing a car, (6) Disadvantages of NOT purchasing a car. He wrote down questions and answers to pertinent questions for each column and came up with the following ideas, his own ideas:

(1) A new car will make me feel good.
A new car will have no maintenance for a long time.

(2) A new car will cost me more. I must find out how long I pay those monthly payments, and if there are penalties if even one is missed. I'll have to buy a license, get a driver's license, and pay insurance. There'll be a big depreciation that first year.

(3) A good used car already has had its big depreciation.
A good used car costs less—I'll still have to check prices.

(4) A used car probably will need repairs sooner.
    I'll still have to buy a license, get a driver's license, and
    pay insurance.

(5) I can save money by riding the bus.

(6) It's inconvenient riding a bus.

The student had many questions, but he felt much more confident when he made the decision to purchase a used car. He also decided to look around more, realizing that he had the choice, that he could get the answers he was looking for by asking questions.

The exercise prompted him to bring in more "reading material"—ads from the paper, the driver's manual, a sample insurance policy. He questioned nearly everything, finding more confidence in himself as he looked for answers, knowing he'd have a choice of which option to choose.

When you help your students develop critical thinking skills in reading, you enable them to transfer these skills to decision making in their lives.

Retention

Many students have mastered the basics of reading but want help in retention of what they've read. They sometimes read word-by-word. Then one unknown word throws them and they stop, forgetting the theme of the story. Here's one suggestion that you might want to try.

1. Together pick a story or a short book of special interest to your students.

2. Ask the students to read one or two paragraphs of the story silently.

3. If students come to words they cannot read, suggest that they skip them and go on. They might want to note unknown words and later look them up in a dictionary, but not while they're reading the story.

4. Ask your students to close the book. Ask one to tell you in one sentence what the paragraph was about.

5. You write down what he or she said.

6. Have your students continue silent reading, paragraph by paragraph. Have them paraphrase aloud what they read, as you continue to write down their words.

7. At the end of the story, ask a student to read the recorded sentences. This is basically an outline of the paragraphs they read.

8. As your students become familiar with this process, suggest that they paraphrase each paragraph by actually saying aloud what they read. Or students can write down one sentence paraphrased from each paragraph. Eventually, students could complete a chapter in a short book and then jot down when they read.

By focusing on the themes within the story, by saying aloud those thoughts, by seeing the paraphrasing in writing, students will in all probability not only understand better but remember what they read.

Using these notes, suggest that your students can write their own versions of the story or book if they wish. That's really writing a short report of that story or book.

Here is an example:

Three young men with limited reading and writing abilities were in my small group. Their problem was reading word-by-word, stopping when they didn't know one word, then re-reading the story. They had concentrated so hard on the unknown words that they'd forgotten the story.

I described several stories and short books, and they chose to read *Jonathan Livingston Seagull,* by Richard Bach.

As they read silently, they'd occasionally say they couldn't read a specific word. I suggested they skip the word and continue reading, telling them they'd probably get the drift of the story without that word. At the end of the first two paragraphs, I asked them to tell me what they read. They were surprised and delighted to find that they could do that. I wrote down their words.

Here are the first seven paragraphs of *Jonathan Livingston Seagull* that they read:[1]

1. "It was morning, and the new sun sparkled gold across the ripples of a gentle sea.

2. "A mile from shore a fishing boat chummed the water, and the word for Breakfast Flock flashed through the air, till a crowd of a thousand seagulls came to dodge and fight for bits of food. It was another busy day beginning.

3. "But way off alone, out by himself beyond boat and shore, Jonathan Livingston Seagull was practicing. A hundred feet in the sky he lowered his webbed feet, lifted his beak, and strained to hold a painful hard twisting curve through his wings. The curve meant that he would fly slowly, and now he slowed until the wind was a whisper in his face, until the ocean stood still beneath him. He narrowed his eyes in fierce concentration, held his breath, forced one... single... more... inch... of... curve... Then his feathers ruffled, he stalled and fell.

4. "Seagulls, as you know, never falter, never stall. To stall in the air is for them disgrace and it is dishonor.

5. "But Jonathan Livingston Seagull, unashamed, stretching his wings again in that trembling hard curve—slowing, slowly, and stalling once more—was no ordinary bird.

6. "Most gulls don't bother to learn more than the simplest facts of flight—how to get from shore to food and back again. For most gulls, it is not flying that matters, but eating. For this gull, though, it was not eating that mattered, but flight. More than anything else, Jonathan Livingston Seagull loved to fly.

---

1 Reprinted with the permission of Scribner, a Division of Simon & Schuster, Inc., from *Jonathan Livingston Seagull* by Richard Bach. Copyright © 1970 by Richard D. Bach and Leslie Parrish-Bach. All rights reserved.

7. "This kind of thinking, he found, is not the way to make one's self popular with other birds. Even his parents were dismayed as Jonathan spent whole days alone, making hundreds of low-level glides, experimenting."

Here are their sentences, paraphrased from their reading of the first seven paragraphs:

Paragraphs 1 and 2:	A fishing boat threw out fish, and seagulls came to eat.
Paragraph 3:	Jonathan Seagull practiced flying and stalling.
Paragraphs 4 and 5:	Jonathan was not an ordinary bird.
Paragraph 6:	Eating is important to most birds, but flying is important to Jonathan.
Paragraph 7:	Friends and parents didn't like Jonathan's experimenting.

One of the young men, still in school, said, "I think I could write a book report now. Never could do that." Another one said, "I thought I had to read every word and that's impossible for me." The third said, "Oh, good! When my little brother asks what I'm reading, I think I can do that. Usually I tell him to forget it and read it himself."

I gave each a copy of the book to read at home. They not only enjoyed the book but couldn't wait to tell me the entire story at our next lesson. No, they didn't write a sentence for each paragraph, but they did say a sentence aloud after each paragraph, paraphrasing what they'd read. They now have confidence in remembering, in retaining what they read. Each knows he could write a report if he ever needed to.

FLUENCY IN READING

Some students want to read aloud to their children. Others want to be able to read directions aloud as they work on a joint project, and yet others want to read a text as they lead a group discussion or from the pulpit of a church or synagogue. But many new readers are hesitant to read aloud. Often it's because previous experiences have been negative. They have had little practice and know their reading aloud just doesn't flow smoothly. They're embarrassed.

However, hearing your students read aloud can provide you with information on their comprehension and word attack strategies. Except during a formal assessment task, suggest that students read silently before reading aloud. Don't hesitate to have them reread a passage several times until they feel comfortable with the material.

As students come to words they stumble over, quietly supply the words and allow them to continue. When students have to wrestle with individual words, they become so busy concentrating on a particular word that they often lose sight of the meaning of the sentence or paragraph. To avoid interfering with the flow of the material, merely supply the word and move on.

Here are some ways to help students develop fluency.

Modeled Reading

Increase students' fluency in reading aloud by modeling, letting them hear how reading flows in phrases, like spoken language. Spend ten minutes or so at the end of each lesson reading to your students. Don't ask comprehension questions afterward. Just let them enjoy and reflect.

Silent Reading Following a Leader

Another effective exercise is to give students copies of material to be read and suggest that they follow the words and read silently as you read aloud or play a tape. As they gain confidence in reading aloud, ask individual students to read aloud as you and/or other students follow their reading.

Choral Reading

It's helpful to you and to the students—whether in one-to-one, small groups, or in classroom settings—to read aloud together. Have copies of the same reading material, so that each of you can follow the reading. Some students may join in softly at first, not sure of their reading. You set the pace, reading slowly enough for them to keep up but fast enough not to distort the meaning. A joint effort that doesn't point out any individual student's weaknesses, choral reading can be a learning experience that builds self-confidence.

Home practice in choral reading could include asking students to read and listen to text at the same time. They can get the rhythm of reading aloud by reading along with good readers, live or recorded.

Impress or Shadow Reading

This exercise can follow choral reading. Tell students that you will all read together, but that you will gradually fade out, or fade in, allowing the individual or small group to take leadership. You might want the students to run their index fingers under the words in their copies of the text as they're reading, keeping the pace set even if occasional "errors" are made. As students become proficient with a selection, reduce the volume of your own voice and gradually become silent. But continue the finger movements under the words so that the students maintain the pace.

You can get the feel of how much reinforcement is needed, gradually lowering your voice to give them confidence that they can read aloud fluently.

Phrase Reading

The degree to which learners can be fluent in reading may well determine the degree to which they comprehend reading material. As you introduce material to students, read it in units of meaning (phrases, clauses, sentences). Intonation patterns in your oral reading will provide students with additional "clues" for comprehension.

For learners who are reading word-by-word, block off phrases in the materials being used:

> **Most work / is done well / when people are happy / and know their jobs.**

Use reading material within the students' reading abilities. The goal is that students recognize how reading flows in phrases.

VOCABULARY

Vocabulary includes all the words of a language, spoken or written. Most of our students have much larger speaking vocabularies than reading or writing vocabularies. They want and need to enlarge the number of words they can read and write.

How do you add new words to your vocabulary? Do you refer to a list of unknown words, disciplining yourself to look up the meaning of five new words a day? No, most people usually add to their vocabularies just by living in a world in which language is used. Even as you read for fun, you don't stop and look up the meaning of each new word. You're too intent on the story; you can't stop. And by the time you've read that new word two or three times, the meaning has usually become clear. You've added a new word to your vocabulary.

Just so with your students. They automatically add to their vocabularies as they read. If, however, the meaning of a word doesn't become clear in the context of the reading material, suggest that they jot down unknown words and guess at their meaning. Then they can look the words up in a dictionary to see if they were right.

There are many ways to teach new words. Because we tend to group or categorize words, it's helpful to teach new words in groupings according to interest or need (e.g. tools, cooking items, words needed in forms to be filled out, medical directions). Teaching words within a family setting, a job-related setting, or a recreational setting quickly leads to words that will be used. You might suggest that students try to decode the words themselves, using the consonant sounds and patterns they know as clues. Or you might teach some of the words as sight words. But be sure your students know the meanings of those new words as you teach them.

Here's one effective way to teach a new word:

1. Write the word in manuscript and say the word.

   employer

2. Ask your students to divide the word into parts or syllables. As they say each syllable, ask them to write syllables, looking at the word for correct spelling.

   em-ploy-er

3. Ask your students if they know the meaning of the word. If not, you give a simple meaning. If your students are interested, show them how to look it up in the dictionary.

   "An employer is the person who hires you to do a job."

4. Put the word in a sentence.

   "The employer of the XYZ Company listens to his workers."

5. Have your students put the word in a sentence.

   "Our employer helps us when we need help."

6. Ask your students to write the word, saying it slowly as they write.

   employer

When asking your students to read a new text, you might pre-teach new words, or you might suggest they skip words they don't know, read on, and get the words and their meanings from the context. Encourage your students to use a dictionary and to use alternate words having the same or similar meanings.

Teaching prefixes and suffixes (e.g. *ex-, un-, pre-, -able*) helps students add new words to those they already know.

You can help students "own" new words by having them read a new word aloud several times, put it in a sentence, spell it, and write it. Many students enjoy keeping their own personal new word lists, adding words as they learn them.

A larger reading and writing vocabulary adds to the enjoyment of reading. It will also help students understand more difficult texts.

SUMMARY

Comprehension is basic to literacy, to reading and writing, to listening and speaking. As a tutor, you need to know when comprehension is taking place and how to help students help themselves as they learn to use comprehension strategies. Increased fluency and a growing vocabulary add to self confidence and promote self image. Students who become more self-directed and independent as they search for information and construct meaning feel successful.

WRITING

ONE OF THE THEMES OF THIS BOOK is viewing language as a whole—listening, speaking, reading, and writing—as mediated through thinking. Furthermore, successful teaching programs recognize that the best teaching occurs when these language components are not taught in isolation. Though this chapter is about writing, a great deal of emphasis is given to reading, speaking, and listening as they relate to the writing process.

In this chapter you will find a general discussion of the process writing cycle as well as specific examples using this cycle in two lessons for goal setting: one in a one-to-one situation with a beginning level student and the other with a group of intermediate students.

Writing is one approach to problem solving. It doesn't just happen in a tutoring session; it happens every day—in families, at work, and in social settings. A collaborative writing process can be used whether you teach in a one-to-one situation, in a small group, or in a classroom setting. Because the writing process constantly requires reading of material being generated, it helps reinforce reading ability. It is never too soon to begin writing activities.

THE WRITING PROCESS

Whoever said there's nothing new under the sun was right; or, at least, there's nothing new about process writing except its name. We have all gone through the process at one time or another.

Think of a time when you bought something, an expensive watch, for example, and it didn't work. What did you do?

Chances are, you fussed and fumed at whoever would listen. You and another person or small group of people talked about the options you had. You might have decided to write a letter of complaint or call the Better Business Bureau. If you called, you probably practiced what you were going to say before you made your call. If you wrote, you probably drafted a letter, read it to and discussed it with someone else, fixed it, rewrote it, read it, until you and your audience were satisfied, and then you sent that letter on its way.

When we have problems, we often solve them through discussion, writing, reading, more discussion, and rewriting. Have you ever solved a problem in this manner? If so, you have used the same steps that make up process writing.

Process writing, which emphasizes discussion, reading, and writing in collaboration with another person or a small group, is often just a way to solve a problem.

The writing process can be broken down into broad parts for the purpose of discussion. (Process writing, the writing process, and the writing cycle are three terms that are used interchangeably throughout this chapter as well as in professional and scholarly journals.)

This process should not be viewed as a lock-step procedure. It may be helpful to think of the steps in the writing process as floors of a building. You can take the elevator from the basement to the third floor and up to the fourth. In other words, you can move up or down, can revisit floors, can go back to the bottom and start over.

In fact, many professional writers frequently move back and forth between steps as they add and delete details, reorder the sequence of information, edit for mechanics, or put a piece away to be dealt with at another time.

The following illustrates how the steps fit into the lesson structure.

The Writing Process

1. **Select trigger event**
2. **Prewrite**
   a. Discuss
   b. Set the writing task
   c. Brainstorm
3. **Write**
4. **Read and respond**
5. **Revise/rewrite**
6. **Edit/rewrite**

Step 1. Select Trigger Event

The trigger event is what starts the discussion. It can be in print (e.g., a story that you read to the students or the students read together) but it doesn't have to be. In fact, it can be just about anything—a picture, a movie, a piece of art work, the local news, a topic of general concern, a problem, or a meaningful experience. Trigger events are usually more successful in prompting discussion if they are of interest to the student or the group and if they are phrased as specific questions.

For example, "What experience or person has had an impact on your life?" or "Have you any interests or concerns you'd like to talk about?" would probably bring up a more effective trigger event for discussion than "What would you like to talk about?" The students then would have a specific question to respond to, a question that evokes a positive, emotional response.

In the first meeting, the tutor may want to set the trigger event. Later, this could be the responsibility of the student or the small group. For a small group formed for a particular purpose (e.g., getting a driver's license, reading to children), the focus of the group will help determine the trigger event.

Step 2. Prewrite

Prewriting includes all those activities that come before the writer begins to draft a piece of writing. These include a good deal of discussion, brain-storming about topics, thinking about logical ways of presenting ideas, making notes or outlines, and narrowing topics into specific and manageable tasks. In this stage writers need to determine their purpose and audience. They need to clarify why they are writing and to whom.

Step 2a. Discuss

To start a conversation and let ideas flow, the tutor asks questions regarding the trigger event.

In this situation, the trigger event often points to student goals. The tutor asks questions about the trigger event to prompt discussion. Ask, don't tell. If you use a movie or video, the trigger question to start a discussion could be, "Well, what do you think?" or "What characters made the biggest impression on you and why?" If the trigger event focuses on student concerns or goals, the questions might be, "Why would changing _____ make a difference to you or your family?" or "What do you need to help you move forward on this?" You are looking for questions that will produce responses of more than one or two words (open-ended responses). Once you elicit the responses, then ask, "Why?" or "Could you tell me more about that?"

Step 2b. Set the Writing Task

Move from discussion to a specific writing task: "Shall we write a letter, book/movie review, a story, a poem?" Or perhaps the writing task could be a report for work.

Step 2c. Brainstorm

Brainstorming is, again, the open-ended process of getting ideas out and bandying them about. Begin with a broad question focused on the writing task: "What might we say about . . . ?"

As you brainstorm together to answer that question, it is helpful to jot down key words, words that will remind the students of specific things they have talked about. This list of key words can serve as a first outline of the writing.

To expand and explain the key words and how they connect, a mapping (or clustering) strategy can be used. This can be done at the brainstorming stage as well as later at a rewriting stage. Mapping helps students put additional ideas on their writing subjects into words, seeing how and where they can expand their key words and ideas. From the key words, have the students say what comes to mind as they reread each word, jotting down the new words as an extension of each key word. You might suggest that your students write these key words on sticky notes so they can be moved around more easily.

For example, suppose parents want to write a letter about their concern for the local schools. Their key phrases might be: *support school, children suffer,* and *education to get jobs.* Mapping could look like this diagram.

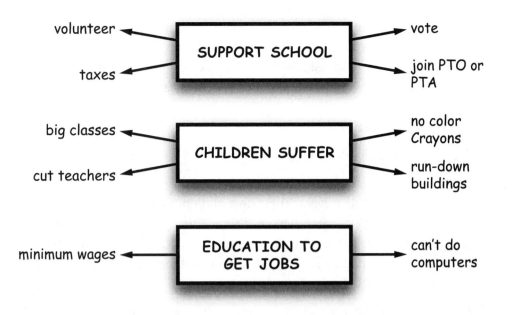

As a tutor, a facilitator of discussion, you can write the trigger event, the task, and the key words as a rough outline on the board, a flip chart, or even a piece of paper, so you may more easily refocus students' thinking on the task when necessary. More advanced students may want and should be encouraged to do their own writing.

The purpose of this brainstorming is to help participants—students and tutors—clarify their own thinking. They have come up with a task, something very specific that they want to accomplish in their writing, and the brainstorming session helps them focus on what they want to do, what they want to say, how they want to say it, and to whom and why they plan to write. Together you are using the spoken language in a very meaningful way, as together you seek to tackle a task, to solve a problem.

Step 3. Write

The students write to get a first draft based on the brainstorming ideas.

The student or the group has figured out what to say and how they want to say it. Now the tutor says, "Our task is on the board or on the paper. We've brainstormed about what we want to say. We even have some of the key words written down. Let's flesh out the writing to get all our ideas down on paper." Encourage the learners to write the best they can; if they cannot spell words, have them write as they think they might be spelled, or write a first letter and draw a line (m____). Assure them that no one else will see their writing.

Because new writers can have difficulty concentrating on all aspects of the written language at one time, experience and research show that you should postpone discussion of editing procedures (spelling, capitals, punctuation, verb forms) until students have written drafts. You want writers to concentrate first on getting their ideas down on paper. After writers have written something, then you can go back and look at spelling, grammar, and mechanics.

You may still have a reluctant writer; in fact, you may be a reluctant writer yourself. The students have talked through their ideas already, so it may be helpful for you to say, "We said it. Now we can write it." Suggest that your students write on every other line, leaving space to edit and revise.

Step 4. Read and Respond

The students read the written material out loud to help clarify what they have written.

In this step, writers will serve as their own audiences as they read for review what they, as well as their peers, have written. Writers should read their work silently and then aloud to themselves; then they should read to the tutor, writing partner, or small group. Reading aloud can be intimidating at first, but it is important for several reasons:

First, it shows students the close relationship between reading and writing.

Second, most native English speakers know when something does not sound right. We might not understand exactly why, but our ears are trained through life experiences to know what "sounds right."

Third, as listeners to our own reading—and readers of our own writing—we become more aware of audience, and we can catch and correct things that don't sound right to us.

To promote discussion after listening, you can establish this routine for both one-to-one and small group tutoring: Ask each person to make at least one positive comment on the writing and pose one clarification question to the writer. Sample questions include:

- What did you mean by…?
- Could you tell me more about…?
- Could you describe…?
- What happened after…?
- What else would you like to add…?

Step 5. Revise/Rewrite

The writers go back to the piece of writing and make changes, usually to answer questions from their own, the tutor's, or their peers' reviews of it. Students might need to add details, use stronger verbs, put things in a logical sequence, add descriptive words, or delete repetitions and/or unnecessary or unwanted parts.

Revision generally concerns content or structure, whereas editing deals with mechanics (spelling, punctuation, capitalization, etc.). If the students are working on computers, this revision process is very easy. Every copy—first draft, second draft, final product—is indeed a printed page. If not, writing on every other line of the page will help. That way, students can add words, phrases, or sentences without too much trouble.

For various reasons, the revision stage of the process is often the one at which the students respond slowly. Remember that the actual physiological act of writing is sometimes painful to students who have never developed the fine motor skills used in writing. Erasures are often messy. Students can be embarrassed by the appearance of their work. Reassure the new writers, letting them know they can rewrite a little later if they "mess up" their pages by revising them. The difficult part is getting their ideas on paper, and they've already done that.

Step 6. Edit/Rewrite

The editing step in process writing helps each student work on the "skills" part of writing. This step also helps you tailor your instruction to each student's needs.

In this step, the writers pay attention to grammar, usage, and the mechanical aspects of writing (spelling, capitals, punctuation, etc.). Even with a three-word sentence by a very beginning writer, for example, the focus could be on beginning a sentence with a capital letter or capitalizing the first letter in a proper name and ending a sentence with a period.

Don't spend much time on editing in early lessons. Writers are often sensitive about errors, and they need encouragement to write. Even suggestions for improvement can be construed as criticism, so tread softly. People may mistake discussions about the errors in their papers for attacks against their personalities. Since many people are frightened of exposing themselves on paper, you want to defuse their fears. Look for patterns of errors and note them in your students' assessment portfolios (folders of selected writing samples, attendance, books and stories read, etc.).

Editing is the most sensitive part of this cycle. As the writers become more confident, they will be better able to deal with constructive criticism. Remind your students that every writer has an editor, sometimes himself, sometimes another person. The amount of editing may depend on the intended audience. For example, a letter to the Board of Education should be as nearly perfect as possible. Something written for one's own use could be more casual.

After a few sessions, encourage writers to be their own editors. Encourage members of the small group to ask each other questions about spelling, grammar, usage, and punctuation.

Keep copies of each student's writing in a separate portfolio. After each session, go over your notes. These will help you plan individual practice and activities for each writer. Note the length of the written pieces as well as the frequency and the types of errors made. Note also the positive aspects of the writing: nice use of details, good organization, clarity of expression, varied vocabulary words, clear descriptions, etc.

For your purposes as a tutor, look at student writings to see patterns of strengths as well as needs. Your assessment of student strengths and needs should guide your instruction. If you find, for example, that a writer has a particularly strong ability to structure an essay into logical order, note this in the writer's portfolio. If not, you can discuss structure or organization of ideas with the student and suggest that the student do some work dealing with organization in class or for home practice. If you see that spelling is not a problem for a particular writer, make that note in the student's portfolio and don't assign extra work on spelling. If you see that the student uses capitals but uses them erratically, note this pattern in the portfolio. Then, work with the student on capitalization in the part of the lesson devoted to reinforcing activities or assign work for home practice.

Be careful not to overwhelm a new student with too many corrections. Work on the most obvious problems. For example, if the student writes a paragraph with every single verb form used incorrectly, work on verbs, not every other error in the paragraph. Students may see writing as a punishment. You want to help change that attitude. While grammar and mechanics are certainly important to the process, they are merely one step. We don't expect our students to become proficient readers overnight; neither should we expect them to become proficient writers overnight. This type of instruction, which comes from the assessment of each individual, is effective because it is learner centered.

Students writing on computers can have a final draft in a matter of minutes. If your students do not have access to computers, your typing the final draft can give them a boost. When texts are typed, they look more like the print students see in books. If you don't have access to a computer, then write the texts carefully in manuscript. Of course, you can also suggest students recopy their own final drafts.

At regular intervals, discuss each writer's progress using examples from the portfolio. It's encouraging, for example, to say, "Mario, your first writing was three sentences long. Look how much more fluent you have become in your writing. You wrote a half-page on this latest project. You're really making progress."

Step-by-Step—The Writing Process

1. Select trigger event
2. Prewrite
   a. Discuss
   b. Set the writing task
   c. Brainstorm
3. Write
4. Read and respond
5. Revise/rewrite
6. Edit/rewrite

We have discussed this process as it relates to tutoring in general. The following is a very specific discussion of how you can use the writing process with beginning or intermediate students, in one-to-one or group settings.

WRITING PROCESS—BEGINNING-LEVEL STUDENTS

You can use this writing model with very beginning-level students as well as with advanced students. Consider the following example:

Step 1. Select Trigger Event

The trigger event starts the discussion. In this example, Chuck Meadows walked into his first tutoring session and said he wanted to learn to read and write to pass a test at work.

Step 2. Prewrite

Step 2a. Discuss

The discussion in this case centered on the test. The tutor discovered that Chuck had dropped out of school after five years because he had to work. The tutor asked him to write his name and address. He wrote his first name but asked the tutor to write his last name. He was unsure of how to write it. The tutor asked, "Chuck, are you unsure of writing or spelling your last name?" "Both," Chuck replied.

At this point, the tutor knew that the written part of the test at work was probably not going to be a realistic goal for Chuck to accomplish in the near future. She also sensed that if Chuck could set and accomplish some smaller goals, he might feel better about himself.

Step 2b. Set the Writing Task

The tutor helped Chuck set the task: "Why do you want to pass the test? If you could tell me why, maybe we could set some short-term goals."

Step 2c. Brainstorm

The task was set in the form of a question; the brainstorming centered on answering that question. Chuck explained that he could not be promoted unless he could write reports about the various work stations in his area. He had been at his job for ten years: he worked hard, everybody respected his knowledge, but he couldn't read. He could not write either. He could not even write his last name.

Step 3. Write

Ordinarily, after the tutor had discussed goals with a potential student, that student would have been asked to write the goals and the writing would have been saved in the student's portfolio. After Chuck had revealed to the tutor he couldn't write his last name, the tutor decided that would not be the best approach. Instead, the tutor asked him, "If you could write anything, what would you write?"

Actually, the tutor thought Chuck would say he'd like to write his whole name. However, Chuck's response was, "Chuck Meadows is a mighty good worker."

The tutor and Chuck made seven word cards, with each word in the sentence on its own card. Chuck could spell three of the words: *Chuck, is,* and *a.* The tutor spelled the other four words as Chuck wrote. Then, the two practiced making sentences with the words, using the word cards:

> Chuck is a worker.
> Chuck Meadows is a good worker.
> Chuck is a mighty good worker.

Chuck wrote these sentences in his notebook, transferring each sentence from the word cards.

Step 4. Read and Respond

Chuck had said all the words, he had generated the sentences, so now he read his sentences aloud. The tutor asked, "Do you want to say more?" Chuck replied, "Not today I don't."

The tutor's response to Chuck was that she was proud he had done so much at the first lesson. She also called attention to the fact that "Meadows" had been included in the sentence, so Chuck could practice writing his entire name now.

Step 5. Revise/Rewrite

There was none in this situation.

Step 6. Edit/Rewrite

The tutor called Chuck's attention to capitalizing the first letters of proper names. This editing lesson was appropriate since two of the seven words were names.

WRITING PROCESS—INTERMEDIATE STUDENTS

Four intermediate-level reader/writers, maintenance workers in the Bates Garment Factory, were requested to write a report to their supervisor. The management was working to improve the company by setting quality management standards, involving all the departments. They needed the help and suggestions from these custodial employees.

Discussions and brainstorming produced the following key words, with their own creative spelling. Mapping expanded their ideas.

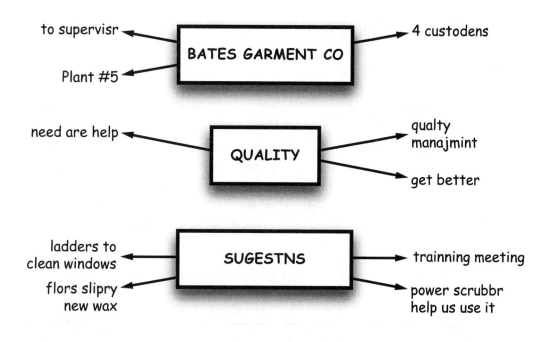

All four group members talked. One man volunteered to draft. He also volunteered to read the first draft to the group. For their second draft, they decided they needed more details.

Because the report had to be sent that day, the workers asked the tutor to correct the spelling on the second draft.

No other help was given. The tutor typed the report, which was sent to the supervisor as follows:

```
To the supervisor
Bates Garment Company, Plant #5

We are happy to help the plant get better
by getting quality management. We are 4
custodians and we need more ladders to
clean the windows. The floors are slippery.
We need new wax and a power scrubber.
Show us how to use it. And we want more
training meetings.

Thank you,

Bill Morgan
Roger Mc Mann
John Anderson
Roberto Herrera
```

MECHANICAL ASPECTS OF WRITING

Handwriting

It is most important that you be familiar with both manuscript and cursive writing before you start to teach students. We usually start with manuscript writing because it seems to be easier for new writers. It also resembles the letters the new readers will encounter in print, leading to a situation in which reading and writing reinforce each other. Since most forms and applications require that the person filling them out do so by printing, learning manuscript writing provides learners with a practical, immediately applicable skill.

Cursive writing may be taught after your students have learned manuscript writing. In cursive writing the letters are connected. Sometimes this connectedness is helpful to poor readers who have trouble keeping a word together. To teach yourself the two recommended alphabets, practice manuscript and cursive alphabets using the sample in the Appendix (see page 170) as a model. Remember these are models only: be consistent, and use upper and lower case as appropriate.

Sam Davis had learned to write his name in manuscript as he learned the letters. It was a milestone for him and he "signed" most of his papers with manuscript letters. One day he came with a specific request. Would the tutor teach him to write his name "the way others write their names"? The tutor had not felt Sam was ready for cursive writing, but "ready" is when a learner really wants to do something. So she showed him how to connect the letters.

As he worked laboriously on his name, he explained that when he signed his name "the other way" (in manuscript), the signature was sometimes questioned and often needed to be verified. It was embarrassing. But even more important, next week was the PTA meeting, and he wanted more than anything else to be able to "sign in" as the other parents did.

Some students aren't interested in writing because they have such poor motor skills; their fingers just don't work well with thin pens or pencils. There are pens that are thicker so that even arthritic fingers can manipulate them. If you can't find a thicker pen, you might try wrapping layers of rubber bands about two inches from the point of the pen. This gives the students more to grab.

What if a student has no interest in learning cursive? That's fine. Do not be surprised to find that your students will progress at a faster rate in reading than in writing. And do not keep your students back in reading because of an inability to write or spell all the words in that lesson. Keep moving ahead in reading, but continue practicing the writing used in earlier lessons. Writing is also an excellent way to review a lesson.

Spelling

Because spelling is important to writers, you may want to teach it in some portion of your lessons. However, it is most appropriate for students to practice spelling the words that come out of their writings at home. Students need to know that they will have to practice spelling individual words if they want to really "own" those words.

When students are unsure of how to spell a word, suggest that they write it as they think it should be, or write the first letters followed by a line (sp____) so that they don't lose their train of thought. As they review their work and want help on specific words, how can you help?

When students ask for help in spelling specific words, you could suggest that they:

1. Write the word one or two different ways to see which one looks right. Seeing it written down often triggers a correct spelling (*deep, depe, deap*).

2. Spell the word aloud to check which spelling sounds right.

3. Think of another word in the same pattern, rhyming with the word. (*Bright,* the problem word, rhymes with *sight.* If they know the beginning letters, *b, r,* and know that *sight* ends in *-ight,* they may come up with the correct spelling.)

4. Refer to other print material to see how it is spelled.

5. Look it up in the dictionary. If the students have no dictionary handy and if trial writings and spellings fail, you can always give the correct spelling.

6. Ask other members of the group. A real change in attitude occurs when group members begin to see each other as resources.

As another way to help your students gain ownership of specific words, you might suggest that they write problem words several times, with intervening attempts to recall the correct spelling following this model:

1. Say the word while looking at the word spelled correctly.

2. Write the word, saying it while writing.

3. Cover the models and write the word again, saying it while writing.

4. Refer again to the model. If the word is correctly spelled, cover the model and write the word again. If spelled incorrectly, refer again to #1, 2, and 3, looking for syllable breaks or patterns, and checking until the spelling is correct.

5. After a lapsed time, perhaps 10 to 15 minutes, write the word again. If it is correctly spelled, the word is probably known. If it is incorrect, some type of review would be indicated.

Sometimes students may need to have correct spelling at once. They may be writing letters or reports that must be mailed that day, and they don't want the embarrassment of incorrect spelling. Just as the spelling checker on a computer gives instant correct spellings, you can give your students the same help. While you don't want to intimidate students by focusing on every incorrectly spelled word, you must honor their requests for instant help as well.

One way to give the correct spellings when requested by students, yet let the writers retain the right to change or not change those words, is to underline each misspelled word carefully and put a number above it. On another page, not on the text, write the correct spelling of each word with a corresponding number.

Students then have the option of rewriting their text and correcting spelling. These misspelled words, too, create a personal word list which can be reviewed for spelling in later lessons.

You might want to give students a chance to point out those words they think are not spelled correctly. They might have their own ideas of strategies to correct the spelling. In small groups, students often help each other with spelling.

Spelling can be an independent area of learning for students, or it can be part of your work together. You may want to suggest that your students develop personal spelling lists.

Capitalization, Punctuation, Grammar

Even new writers must learn when and where to capitalize letters and what punctuation to use where. Early on, you'll probably explain that the name of a person or place as well as the first word in a sentence or question starts with a capital letter, that sentences end with periods, and that questions end with question marks. Commas, semicolons, colons, exclamation marks, and other punctuation marks are more complex. You might want to check your library or local book store for more detailed help.

There are many books to help your students when they need help in grammar—in understanding rules of nouns, verbs, adverbs, adjectives, etc. Check them out at your local book store or library to be sure they're simply written so that your students can understand them.

SUMMARY

As you think about writing and the tutoring of writing, consider the following:

- Your definition of writing might not be the same as your students'. Writing is primarily the creation of a text for a particular purpose and audience. It also includes sub-skills and editing skills like handwriting, grammar, spelling, and punctuation.
- You may or may not go through a whole writing cycle with every student at every session. The important thing is to include some reading, some writing, some listening, and some speaking at each lesson. You will see that most students learn faster when language components are presented in an integrated rather than an isolated manner.

- Not all writing needs the same degree of revising and editing. One would revise a grocery list to make sure all items are included, but would probably not correct spelling or rewrite for neatness. One would be more careful and detailed about a letter to a prospective employer.

- Students may say they don't need to know how to write. What do they need to write? Novels, poems, plays, short stories? Probably not. How about notes, appointments, lists, letters, checks? That's writing also. In a learner-centered situation, you will want to help students identify their own writing needs.

- Many programs are publishing student writings. Seeing one's own words in print in a bound publication is a great incentive for writing as well as a boost to self-esteem. This project is especially easy if students regularly use the computer for writing at least final drafts.

- It is never too early to start a student on a computer. You might be concerned that the student does not know the keyboard, but the hunt-and-peck method does not distract even beginning students. Actually, using the computer has a positive effect on student self-esteem. Many libraries have computers that can be used by your students.

- If students are really excited about very lengthy stories but their hands cannot move as quickly as their thoughts, you might encourage them to record their stories on tape recorders and take dictation from themselves, regulating the tape to their own speed. Tape recorders are also good for students who can say what they want to write but have a mental block once they try to put pen to paper. They, too, can record their messages and play them back to themselves,

- Everybody has a story to tell, and writing preserves those stories. The written word connects where we've been to where we're going; it preserves our past and looks toward our future. If we view writing in that way rather than as a negative way to record grammar and spelling errors, our students will value it as we do.

IDENTIFYING AND SETTING GOALS

6

DEFINING AND SETTING GOALS are among the most important first activities in any learner/tutor relationship. Motivation for learning to read and write is a prime factor in actually learning these skills. Here are some suggestions for identifying and setting both long-term and short-term goals and for tracking progress. These are important records to share with donors; they can help to meet requirements of funders.

LONG-TERM GOALS

Each student has his or her own goals. They might include getting a GED or high school equivalency, reading a job manual, getting a driver's license, reading and writing letters to loved ones far from home, or reading to children. Because we suggest that all lessons be learner-centered, the tutor must know the students' goals so that these can be the focus of the lessons.

To help you get a feel for your students' goals, discuss them with your students, but also review individual student intake interview forms to refresh yourself on their interests and goals as well as their strengths and needs. Encourage your students to think about their futures, to dream about what they'd like to do in life, where they'd like to be in one year, in five years, even in ten years. Help them identify these goals.

Use the "Learner Goals and Interests" checklist in the Appendix (see pages 171–172) as a starting point for informal discussions with your students about goals. Often students have trouble being specific; they give general goals, such as *"I want to learn to read and write better,"* or *"I want to help my children,"* or *"I want to get a better job."* Asking questions like *"What do you want to learn to read and why?"* or *"How do you want to help your children?"* or *"What kind of a job do you want?"* can supply you with useful information in helping them set their own goals. There are many suggestions within each category that might help your students to focus on more specific goals that can be broken down into objectives and practical lesson plans.

SHORT-TERM GOALS

A long-term goal is a destination—the distant city, the far mountains. Short-term goals are the signposts along the way that help measure progress toward the ultimate goal.

But before you set out on such a journey, you need to analyze just what you have to do to reach your destination. This task analysis results in a list of things to know or do if the goal is to be reached. The translation of goals into objectives is much like making a list of things to do before you take a trip:

☐ Pack the car.
☐ Get money from the bank.
☐ Put gas in the car.

If one of your student's goals is to use a telephone book competently, your list of objectives might look like this:

- ☐ Alphabetize names through three letters.
- ☐ Use guide words on the page.
- ☐ Alphabetize first names.
- ☐ Explain abbreviations used in a phone book.
- ☐ Find categories used in the yellow pages.
- ☐ Find other sources of information in the phone book.

The practical result of a task analysis is the setting of objectives for a particular lesson. What you and each learner will want to accomplish by the end of the lesson determines what you'll teach. For example, if a student wants to be a cook, a short-term goal could be to collect recipes. Being able to write and then to read a recipe could be the objective for one lesson. The recipe could provide the unifying objective for the majority of the activities during that lesson.

SEQUENTIAL GOAL SETTING MODEL

It seems to be difficult for many students to reduce long-term goals into their smaller components. You might want to use the Sequential Goal Setting Model to help you and your students break the long-term goals down into realistic short-term goals and identify the skills needed.

Write down each student's long term goal. Think of this as the top of a ladder. What are the barriers that must be overcome, the steps that must be taken to get from where the student is now to the top of that ladder, to attain that long-term goal? Start from the top and go down, step by step, identifying what your student needs to get to the next step up, until you come to where your student is now, identifying exactly what he/she must do first.

An Example

Melanie dropped out of school when she was 16 having completed the eighth grade. Her children have completed high school. She had encouraged them, and now she wants to do it herself, to get her GED, her high school equivalency. As Melanie discussed it with her teacher, she wrote down what steps she had to take: before she got her GED, she realized she must pass the GED test. In order to pass the GED test, she realized she'd have to go to GED classes to improve her reading and writing. But she realized even this was beyond her at the moment, for she wanted to get a tutor to help her review her basic skills. Her ladder to reach her goal might look like this:

Get my GED

Pass the GED test

Go to GED classes

Improve my reading/writing

Get a tutor to help me review my basic skills

Get help in improving my reading/writing skills

Charles, too, dropped out of school at 16 and was unemployed. He wanted to get a job in maintenance where he knew he could do the work. But he also knew he needed some help. His ladder to reach his goal might look like this, but he must start at the bottom to get to the top.

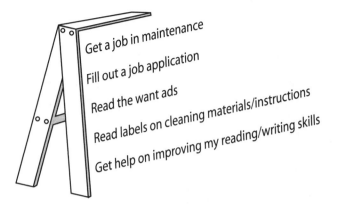

Get a job in maintenance

Fill out a job application

Read the want ads

Read labels on cleaning materials/instructions

Get help on improving my reading/writing skills

Actually seeing their own Sequential Ladders, both Melanie and Charles could see why and what they needed to do to reach their goals. Using the techniques suggested in this book, their tutors or teachers could focus their lessons on what the students identified as their needs.

GOALS SET THROUGH THE WRITING PROCESS

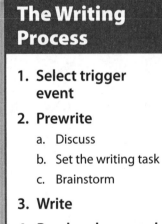

The Writing Process

1. **Select trigger event**
2. **Prewrite**
   a. Discuss
   b. Set the writing task
   c. Brainstorm
3. **Write**
4. **Read and respond**
5. **Revise/rewrite**
6. **Edit/rewrite**

In Chapter 5, you learned how to use the six steps in the writing process. You can use these same six steps to help your students set their goals.

An Example

Step 1. Select trigger event

In this example, the trigger event is the topic of setting goals. You can start the lesson any number of ways. You could introduce the idea of individual goal setting by using printed materials that reflect literacy learners' goals. In *"My Goal,"* by a literacy learner from Kentucky, the author writes that she entered a literacy program for one reason: to read a book to her daughter. Her daughter, who is now in her twenties and has her own child, used to walk around the house, carrying her favorite little book, *The Bunny Rabbit.* When she was little, she'd climb up in her mother's lap, dragging the book with her. Her mother, a nonreader, would point to the pictures and make up stories.

In time, as the little girl started school and became a reader herself, she stopped climbing into her mother's lap, demanding to be read to. No words ever passed between mother and daughter about the subject.

After the daughter married, the mother entered a literacy program. Her goal? To read to her child. On Easter Sunday after the mother had been in a program for over a year, the daughter, now expecting her own baby, came home for a visit. Based on the story, we can imagine that their conversation went something like this:

"Go back in your room and get me your favorite book," the mother said.

"Is it time for me to take it home with me to read to my own baby?" asked the daughter as she returned to the den with *The Bunny Rabbit* in hand.

"No, I plan to keep that book," was the mother's reply. "Here, now, you sit in my lap." The daughter looked at her mother incredulously. "I'm your mother, and I say sit in my lap," repeated the mother. Laughing, the daughter obeyed.

The mother opened the book and began to read, "Once upon a time . . . ." Mother and daughter both burst into tears. After a few minutes, though, the mother asserted herself: "We've got to cut this out. I have waited 25 years to read this book to you, and I intend to do it!"

(This story appears in *Slices of Life: Kentucky Writers for Kentucky Readers*, published by the Lexington, Kentucky, *Herald-Leader*, 1989.)

Step 2.Prewrite

Step 2a. Discuss

After you read or tell the above story, tell the student or the group that the story is true. Then ask, "What did you think of it?" Allow a few minutes for discussion. Encourage reactions to the story.

Then ask, "What was the mother's goal?" Students will probably say, "To read to her little girl" or "To read the book about the bunny rabbit." Then you could say, "As we begin our sessions together, we must figure out our own goals. This woman had a very specific goal that she wanted to accomplish. Her tutoring sessions focused on that goal. What are some of the goals you'd like to accomplish in our time together?"

The trigger event was the story of a mother accomplishing her goal. Encourage the students to discuss some of their goals.

When working with a group to set goals, consider which of the two kinds of groups you are working with: those formed around an announced topic or focus (such as reading with children or improving job performance) or those formed without an announced topic (e.g., you have three people who may not even know each other and want to meet to learn to read better as a small group on Wednesdays and Fridays). The session on goal setting will differ accordingly. The group formed around an announced goal can go right into setting the writing task, Step 2b, after a short discussion to remind everyone of the purpose of the lessons.

Whether you are working with one or several learners, your purpose is the same: to get students talking about goals. You might ask students for a definition of "goal" if you find that they initially have trouble with the concept. This discussion should take only a few minutes, although it is perfectly acceptable to go five or ten minutes, as long as the discussion is focused on goals.

Step 2b. Set the Writing Task

Summarize what has been said.

You might remind them: "In our discussion, we've said there are several goals we'd like to accomplish. We all said we wanted to read and write better. John said he'd like to make more money. Elise said she'd like to be able to talk to her children's teacher without being embarrassed. Marita said she'd like to read better. For this session, let's concentrate on some very specific things we'd like to do."

"Remember the woman in the story? Her goal was to read one specific book to her daughter. Tell me what your goals are and I'll list them on the board, unless you'd like to write them yourselves."

When working with only one student, encourage that learner to be specific on a goal.

Write the task and the discussed goals on the board, a flip chart, or a piece of cardboard or notebook paper. The students should see the words describing the task written down.

Step 2c. Brainstorm

The tutor and students have discussed goals earlier. That discussion was rather broad, concerning the writer of "My Goal," other people they know, and possibly themselves. Now it's time to narrow the discussion to focus on the writing task at hand. Suggest that each participant identify a specific goal.

Your job is to help the students clarify or narrow their goals into manageable short-term goals. For example, it's common for some learners to say, "I just want to learn to read better." Ask, "What do you want to learn to read better? Is there something at work you'd like to read? At home? Some kind of hobby?" Continue to explore their interests and needs.

You might have students who have stated they would like to go into formal adult basic education classes and work toward a high school equivalency diploma. Be sensitive to their feelings as you respond, "That's certainly a worthwhile goal. It might take you a little time though, several years maybe. Let's make that a long-term goal. What would be a specific goal you'd like to accomplish within the next few months that might eventually lead to a diploma?" In the example above, when Marita was questioned about what she wanted to read, she said she'd like to read the inventory items at her work station.

Examples of learner goals are listed in the Appendix on pages 171–172. These can help you as you try to help the students clarify or narrow their individual goals. Do not read lists to the learners; use these examples as suggestions. Lists should not be used as menus. Often, adult learners will fall into the old school mode of choosing one of those items on what they consider "your" list rather than telling you what they really want to do. Again, ask, don't tell. Keep probing through open-ended questions to help students explore or articulate their goals.

If you're working with a group formed around a topic, the group goal is easier to discover: read to children, read the newspaper, get a driver's license, etc. Suggest that group members take two or three minutes and tell at least one specific goal each has set.

It's up to you to set closure on this activity. Give the learners a time limit to keep them secure.

Step 3. Write

After students have articulated their particular goals, the tutor should summarize, signaling the next step.

You might say: "We've shared our goals. Let's take a few minutes and write down at least one or two specific goals."

If the learners are hesitant, assure them that no one else will see their writing without permission. Restate the goal, emphasizing that the students have already talked, now they just need to write.

Here is an example of how one tutor handled this situation.

> **Tutor:** Marita, you said you'd like to read better, specifically to read the inventory items at your work station. You said the words. Now write those words.
>
> **Marita:** How am I supposed to spell *inventory?*
>
> **Tutor:** What else could you call them? What else could you say? "My goal is . . . ?" Finish that sentence another way.
>
> **Marita:** My goal is to read the things at work.
>
> **Tutor:** Great. Now write what you just said, "My goal is to read the things at work."

Step 4. Read and Respond

Suggest that the students read their goals silently. Then ask for volunteers to read their goals aloud.

You will probably want to list your students' goals on the board or on paper. It's a good way to let the students see (and then "read") their goals. You have two options: you can have each student read to you and you write the goals on the board, or you can ask for volunteers to write their own or others' goals on the board. Since this goal setting activity should be done at the first or second tutoring session, it may be less threatening to have them read to you and you write. But, of course, ask, don't tell. You may have someone who likes to write.

It's important to discuss the goals as they appear on the board. Clarification questions should be encouraged. Be sure to reinforce students' work with positive comments. Questions that might bring positive responses could be: "What are particularly clear points?" or "What makes this very easy to understand?"

Learners sometimes select goals that may take a year or more to reach, such as earning a high school diploma or getting a better job. Sometimes they select broad, hard to measure goals such as being a better reader. In these cases, as you respond you might ask the students to help word the goals in such a way that they are more easily measurable and/or attainable. Help them focus by asking direct questions. Suggest they write down something they can see or do. For example, you can't see "a better reader" but you can see someone "reading two books." You can't see "a better job," but you can see someone "reading a want ad."

Step 5. Revise/Rewrite

Encourage the learners to write more or to play around with what they have already written based on the discussion of goals. This is not a tremendous undertaking because you have asked for only two or three goals. With the words already on the board or on paper, learners can correct their own spelling if they wish. Each student has now said, read, and written the words, explaining goals. You have written them correctly as an example.

This is an early session. You might not want to elaborate or further develop the goals. You might want to add comments on the board or easel paper, but not on an individual learner's papers. You might see that the learners have had enough writing for the day. While elaboration or development provides expanded practice with the learners' own writing about goals, use your own developing knowledge of your students to decide when to go to the next step.

If you are working with beginners and asking them to write, one sentence is usually enough. If your learners are more advanced, you probably will get more writing. Let them decide how much to write. The earlier procedure of sharing, commenting, revising, sharing, commenting, and perhaps revising further is then repeated as learners produce their texts:

☐ Learners read their sentences to the group (one-to-one learners read to their tutors).

☐ The group comments. Then the tutor comments and asks clarification questions.

☐ Learners revise based on the comments.

- Learners again read to the group (or to the tutor).

- The group (or one-to-one tutor) again comments.

- Learners may or may not revise further.

You can stop at this point if you or your students seem tired or tense. Be encouraged that the students did some writing.

Step 6. Edit/Rewrite

The purpose of this first or second session has been to set goals for future sessions. You may not have time to do any more editing or rewriting at this time. You have written the goals on paper or on the board. Students may have corrected their own spelling at Step 5 or they may do so now. Students should be encouraged to copy their goals into their notebooks for further reference. The tutor should also copy the goals for individual files.

Remember to keep a portfolio for each student. Ask each student to make a copy of his or her goals for your portfolio. Students keep the originals and give you the copies.

SUMMARY

Having identified their long-term and short-term goals, your students can see a path to success more clearly. They can understand why they need to learn the skills that are missing from their education. And you, the tutor, can focus your lesson plans to help your students reach those goals.

RESOURCES AND ACTIVITIES

Resources
Maps
Calendars
Menus
Other Authentic Materials
Games
Workbooks
Audio Recordings
Technology

Activities
Notes and Lists
Journal Writing
Letters
Alphabetizing
Library Use
Sequencing/Following Directions
Silent Reading
Reading Out Loud

Summary

ONE OF THE FIVE THEMES OF THIS BOOK IS IMMEDIATE RELEVANCE; as you provide activities students find relevant, the tutoring sessions will be more productive.

Learning to read and write can be a challenging and satisfying series of successes as you accommodate your students' needs, interests, and capabilities, sensing when to change materials and when to nudge the learners.

The advantage of tailoring tutoring to students is that the students are not committed to a prescribed curriculum. They are spared the necessity of learning material that may be tediously irrelevant to their lives. Your challenge is to locate materials of interest to your specific students.

Because it's rare to find materials for adults neatly categorized into grade levels, we prefer to look at broader groupings that allow for such factors as students' prior knowledge, language, and interests. This chapter will look at resources, materials, and activities relevant to the abilities and needs of your students.

RESOURCES

Maps

If students want to read maps, find out what type of maps they have in mind. You might develop a map of the area where you meet. This strategy allows you and the students to use the "map" to represent a real, known area. If there is a misunderstanding about what the map represents, you have the actual space as a reference.

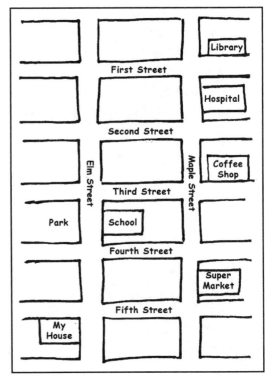

You and your students could walk around the park, neighborhood, city, and beyond. Gradually make the transition of using only a map, letting the students be the guides. New words could be added to your student's personal word list—*north, south, east, west, left, right, turn, highway, street signs, supermarket, hospital, library, gas station.*

Planning a trip—even an imaginary one—can be a lot of fun. The names of cities and states, words on road signs, and words used in directions are all practical words, constantly needed. You might capitalize on your students' interest in certain places. Provide the students with a set of directions that could be followed just by using a standard road map. In addition, using the mileage charts on maps can be an interesting way to incorporate some math into lessons.

A city map can provide an additional source for development of map reading skills. Your students can identify what streets would be traveled to reach the airport, a shopping plaza, or the library.

Calendars

Using a calendar is a valuable skill. It's surprising to find that some students don't understand what a calendar is and how it can be used. When students know that the days of the week are noted at the top, you can explain why the first day of the month is sometimes a Sunday, sometimes a Monday, or another day of the week. Writing the names of the days of the week can be a good spelling lesson, and identifying the sounds of the first letters of each day can reinforce letter-sound relationships.

Remember that learning occurs by doing. Talk with your students about important dates to remember. Practice using the calendar to note meetings, birthdays, doctors' appointments, rent payments, or pay day. A pocket calendar or a page-size monthly calendar simplifies keeping various commitments. Suggest that students write down the days and times of your lessons and other important dates.

Menus

In your constant search for practical materials, don't overlook menus from restaurants, cafes, or diners in the area. You might bring in a few, or ask the students to bring some. Encourage the students to read what they can from these menus. Ask students what they like to eat or what they would like to order. Then teach these words from the menus. You can teach some words as sight words (e.g., *pizza, soup*); teach others by associating them with words already known (e.g., *beef stew, hot dogs*), applying the principles of phonics and patterns.

Other Authentic Materials

Recipe books, food boxes, product labels, health and safety folders, magazines, song lyrics, sales circulars, and travel brochures—all print around you and your students is fair game for lessons. Have students bring in material that they are interested in reading. In this way they can exercise some control over the content of their lessons.

Games

Games can be valuable tools that bring a change of pace to lessons and give the students an opportunity to use the strategies they've been working on. Whether you use games that you purchase or that you create, keep in mind that any game should

- ☐ involve reading and writing.
- ☐ be fun and challenging without frustrating the students.
- ☐ be geared to adult interests and abilities.
- ☐ be played fairly. (Do not allow your students to win if they don't deserve to, but use games that fit the abilities of your students.)

As with many other materials, adapt games to fit the needs of each student. Don't worry about changing the rules; remember that materials are there for your use. Simple crossword puzzles, either from books or devised by you, are fun to do with students. Incorporate words the students are having difficulty with, or perhaps put their own names into the puzzle. Commercially available word games include *Anagrams, Scrabble, Boggle,* and *Spill n' Spell.*

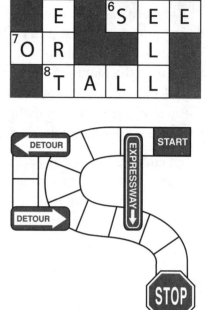

You might invent trail games, letting the students set the destination. Names of cities could be included; road signs (STOP, DETOUR) could be deterrents, and other signs (SPEED LIMIT 55, THRUWAY) could move the traveler more quickly.

A challenging but entertaining way to work on word recognition is to play Word Bingo. On letter-sized sheets of paper or cardboard, draw appropriate lines and write in manuscript some words your students are working on, making each sheet different by mixing the arrangement of the words. Write the same words on a set of cards from which you and your students will draw. Take turns pulling the word cards and reading them as you cover the word on the sheet.

For beginning students, you might use the first 24 words in the Most Frequently Used Words list in the Appendix (see page 191). For more advanced students use more difficult words.

B	I	N	G	O
the	is	and	in	that
of	he	as	his	by
a	for	BINGO	be	I
was	it	this	at	had
on	with	not	are	but

Workbooks

If you use workbooks, it is important not to work through them mechanically page by page, book by book. Instead, always keep your students' goals in mind, interspersing reading and writing events as often as possible.

Audio Recordings

An audio recording can be an excellent educational tool. Although tape recorders are not as common as they once were, they can be very helpful—it is worth looking for them. Some students may have them; if not, your program may have one you can use. In addition, some computers have built-in microphones that make it possible for students to record themselves speaking and then play the recordings back.

A recording of a text provides a model of fluent oral reading and accurate word pronunciation. Students can follow the words while they listen. They can read aloud along with the recording. They can review the material and repeat activities as many times as they please. This lets students have the responsibility for some self-evaluation.

Show your students how to make use of recordings. Then encourage them to work independently. If possible, store recordings of the students' work in their portfolios.

Here are some other ways tutors have found to use recordings as tools:

1. Record your students as each reads aloud. Have the students play back the recordings. They will often spot their own reading problems and seek to correct them.

2. Find out what kinds of music your students like. Use lyrics as a tool for learning to read and write by getting printed copies. Suggest that students read or even sing along with recordings.

3. Make an audio recording of a selection your students find interesting. Provide them with a written copy of the selection. Have each replay the selection, reading along with the recording. This exercise will improve the person's reading fluency.

4. Record a sample of a student's oral reading as you assess progress. Recordings taken at intervals give you a permanent record for later reference and evaluation, and provide evidence of student progress.

5. Record an entire lesson between you and your students. At your leisure, listen to the recording and critique yourself. Are you talking too much? Do you sometimes talk down to your students? Do you give them enough time to respond to questions?

A note of caution: preview any material before you use it with students. Regional accents, loud music, and childish intonation on some commercially-produced recordings make them inappropriate for use with adult students.

Using a recording can be fun, and it provides a change of pace in a lesson. Hearing their own improvement will help give your students confidence in their own abilities.

Technology

There is much excitement about the use of appropriate educational technology in teaching basic reading and writing. Computers can be used both to supplement a tutor's instructions, giving the students opportunities for practice and review and reinforcing the skills you're teaching, and as stand-alone instructional tools. Check out the technology and software resources in the Appendix (see page 205) as well as those in your local library.

There are educational software programs for beginning as well as for more advanced readers. Some programs are more appropriate for basic literacy/adult basic education, and others are designed for English for Speakers of Other Languages (ESOL). If your students have vision problems, you might want to search for programs that scan the printed page and deliver a talking voice. Many programs allow users to change the font, the size, and even the color of text on a computer screen. Speech-to-text and other talking software and devices are available, including talking dictionaries.

Many hesitant writers do not balk at writing on the computer for several reasons. First, poor handwriting often deters writers. Physically, writing can be difficult, even painful, for new writers who may not have developed the fine motor skills needed for neat handwriting. Second, revising and editing are much easier to do on a computer than by hand. Much less physical effort is needed to add details and re-copy, edit, and re-copy. Third, the printed page is pleasant to any reader's eye. New writers often become discouraged and embarrassed if their handwritten papers appear messy. Fourth, programs that check spelling provide another way to reinforce spelling. Finally, the ability to write on a computer is a real boost to students' self-esteem and might even become a pathway to job opportunities.

Using computers for writing should not replace teaching students to write by hand. Everyone has access to a pencil or pen. Most of us are given forms to be filled out on the spot. We all make lists. Certainly you should work on the formation of letters with students. If you and your students have access to a computer, though, don't hesitate to try it. A tutor could introduce a software program (several are listed in the Appendix), and students could progress through that program at their own speed. This can be especially helpful when students are working on writing that will require revising and editing. Making printouts at various stages in the development of a text will allow students to see their actual progress.

Do not think you need to teach handwriting and computer writing at different times. You can begin these two things at the same time. Students do not need to form letters beautifully before they begin to write on the computer. If you are not familiar with computers, you and your students can learn together.

If your literacy program doesn't have a computer, look into using the facilities of a local library, community center, corporation, school, university, or public adult basic education program to see if they would share their computers and their word processing or teaching programs during "off times."

Several available books give detailed directions for using regular word processing, spelling check, and spreadsheet programs to teach reading and writing in an authentic environment.

You can expose your students to the Internet, the Web. Show them how to find information on subjects of particular interest to them. They can quickly learn to type in the words that describe their needs or interests—soccer, recipes, crossword puzzles, whatever—and pick and choose what they want to read.

While software and the Internet offer incredible learning tools for adult literacy students, technology cannot replace volunteer tutors. As we help students connect with the economic, social, and civic lives of their communities, we can extend our ever-growing learning philosophy to include helping them to connect with the "real world" of technology.

ACTIVITIES

Notes and Lists

Notes and lists may be two of the most frequent ways writing is used in our day-to-day living. Discuss the kinds of notes that the students would like to write, then ask each to write a few notes. You will likely get a note to a family member, a shopping list, a list of activities for the day, or a note to a teacher.

Journal Writing

Of the many types of journals, we'll discuss three—private, dialogue, and circular. They are used for different purposes.

Private Journal Writing • Private journal writing appeals to many learners. And it's just that, private. Your students may or may not want you to read what they write. Even if they ask you to read it, make comments or suggestions only on the content, not on the mechanics. Private journals are for the individual student's use. Ask your learners to write at least two sentences a day in a special notebook. They can write about what they did that day or how they felt about the day. They can make comments about the weather or experiences with a friend or family. As students progress, encourage them to write more. Often these two daily sentences will expand to a page or two. Point out that writing—any kind of writing—is also going to help them with reading. Rereading their journals may give them ideas for further writing.

Dialogue Journal Writing • In this type of journal, you also write, responding to what the learners have written. The process continues back and forth. This dialogue leads the learners to rethink and expand on what they have written. Your response will serve as a model for correct grammar, spelling, and punctuation. Reading what you write further develops the learners' language and comprehension skills.

Even very beginning readers and writers are able to use a dialogue journal. The first entries may include pictures or brief written messages. You can respond by writing a nonjudgmental comment. As you write, keep your students' reading proficiencies in mind.

Circular Journal Writing • Journal writing also can be used to write fiction. The tutor starts a story, finishing with a cliffhanger-type sentence, giving it to a student to write the next part. When the student finishes, it goes back to the tutor or other students in the group, and they continue to add on to the story. The tutor, of course, models correct usage and spelling. It's fun, and, for some students, more comfortable than private or dialogue journals because it isn't about their personal lives. Again, over time the students become more creative and write longer passages.

Letters

Letter writing can also be a valuable experience for students. Perhaps you are going on a trip. You can continue your lessons while you are away by writing to your students. Write in manuscript or cursive, depending on the ability of your students, and use words your students know or can figure out. You might also send postcards to your students when you are away. Sending postcards lets people know that you remember them. Postcards also carry a simple personal message that students can read, as well as a picture of a part of the world your students may not have seen.

Suggest that students write to you as well. The first time, it's a good idea to give your students a pre-addressed stamped envelope and a sheet of paper showing how to write a letter. In your lesson, demonstrate how to start a letter and several ways to end a letter.

Writing letters to out-of-town friends or family members can also be motivating and meaningful to many students. One student began corresponding with his grandmother whom he hadn't seen in fifteen years. It not only meant a great deal to him but also provided authentic reading and writing material for lessons.

A personal letter could be:

Dear Mom,

We got to Detroit the first night no trouble with the car weather is great. Will write more tomorrow.

Love,
Richard

One student wrote a more formal letter to her child's teacher:

Dear Mrs. White,

Please send Sharons glasses home today call me if you
need me.

Yours truly
Mrs. Beverly Jackson

You will get a big thrill when you receive your student's letter. It might be the first letter your student has ever written. The spelling may not be perfect, the grammar may not be correct, but you'll know what it means, and that is the important thing.

Alphabetizing

Alphabetizing can be a helpful skill when using a phone book or a dictionary or when searching for a book in the library. Most people can recite the alphabet from memory; if your students cannot, write the letters in order as an easy reference. Explain that dictionaries, telephone books, and files are set up in alphabetical order.

Use a variety of words your students may need to alphabetize, perhaps selecting eight names that start with the first eight letters of the alphabet:

Felipe	David	Anna	Chris
Greg	Bob	Emily	Heather

Put each on a word card and have the students put them in alphabetical order. You could use animals, flowers, or cities, depending on your students' interests. When your students can alphabetize words beginning with all 26 letters, point out that:

A through F would be roughly in the first third of the dictionary.
G through O would be roughly in the middle section.
P through Z would be roughly in the last third.

This guide will be useful as a quick reference for dictionaries.

Some students do not realize that words are put in alphabetical order using the second or third letters when the first or second are the same. Suggest that your students alphabetize the following words: *as, apple, about*. Then have them alphabetize words for which the differing letter is the third one: *bread, bride, brain*. Continue to point out opportunities to alphabetize as they occur in your sessions.

Library Use

Students may be introduced to the public library early in tutoring; in fact, you and your student might be meeting at a local library for your teaching sessions.

You might want to point out the adult new reader section to help your students find books that are of interest and within their range of reading abilities.

Since libraries can be intimidating to some new readers, it is a good practice to make a library visit a part of your lessons. During the first visit, help students get library cards and become familiar with the library's services. It is a good idea to provide or arrange a tour of the library and to point out the variety of materials available. For example, many adults don't know that public libraries have magazines, CDs, and DVDs; reference, business, and voter registration information; computers for public use; and special programs for both children (story hours, movies, and summer reading programs) and adults (movies and speakers). Some libraries even loan framed prints and toys. And some adults don't know that all these library services are free to the public.

During your library tour, review check-out procedures including how to determine when the book is due and how to renew a checked-out book when you need more time. Users of libraries must know that there is a fine for overdue books and that they are responsible for books checked out on their cards. It may be possible to work out an arrangement with the library to allow extra renewals or longer borrowing periods for adult new readers.

Let students know that it is unnecessary to finish a book they don't like. Share some situations in which you have started a book but lost interest in it or found it inappropriate for your own needs. Let them know that you can't judge a book by its cover and that many people initially misjudge books.

Unless there is a special collection of books for adult literacy students, it will be extremely difficult for a low-level reader to find usable books from the confusingly large volume of material available. If your library does not have a special collection for adult beginning readers, urge them to establish one. Ask the librarian to help the students find appropriate picture or simple reading books.

One way to help students through this maze of materials is for tutors to locate several books related to each student's goals and interests. You can help students choose a book by looking at author, title, illustrations, information about the author, table of contents and chapter headings, length, etc. Since not nearly enough books have yet been written specifically for adults with lower reading proficiencies, the next best resource is young adult books. The usable materials are not usually listed in the bibliographies for adult beginning readers, but students tend to be enthusiastic about them. If your program doesn't have a list of these titles, you may have to go on a treasure hunt in the young adult book section. To make certain the material is appropriate, read a little yourself and check the illustrations. Be sensitive; avoid going into the children's section unless the students express a desire to do so or if they are looking for books to read to their children.

The method of locating books in a library is changing. Instead of a card catalog, there may be a computer that the librarian will demonstrate for you. No matter which method is used, you can locate a specific book by author, title, or subject.

Most local libraries have computers that can be used by the public. Your students can reserve times and go at their own speed. With the Internet, the world of materials is wide open.

As students begin to feel comfortable in libraries, they enjoy exploring the different sections. Encourage this exploration.

Sequencing/Following Directions

Even with someone who has limited reading skills, you can work on sequencing skills. Ask your students to respond to two or three verbal directions. For example:

> "Open your book to page 62, and count the number of words in the first five lines."

Something as simple as this exercise can give you information about whether a student can follow directions. It also enables you to determine whether students understand the boundaries between words.

Gradually increase the number and complexity of the directions to which your students are asked to respond. For example:

> "Open your book to page 25. Look at the pictures and then tell me what you think the article is about. After that, let's jot down the key words together."

As a practical exercise and to reinforce aural sequencing, give your students a series of directions typical of those offered to a person looking for a particular house:

> "Go up the hill past the third traffic light. Turn left at the Exxon station, and go to the white house with the red mailbox in front."

See if your students can repeat these instructions in order. Encourage your students to develop a picture in their minds as they listen. This helps to increase the likelihood of following the directions in the right order.

Then move to printed directions. Recipes and how-to-do-it manuals are good sources for practice. The directions on a cake mix box are excellent. Have your students read through the entire sequence of action and then describe or act out the sequence required by the directions. They can refer to the printed directions at any time. The purpose is to keep the directions in the correct sequence.

Another interesting activity is to take a strip of paper and write down a sequence of events:

> In the morning when the alarm clock goes off, I have to get up, get dressed, eat breakfast, and catch a bus before 7:30.

Cut apart each phrase containing one activity or description, and ask your students to reassemble the events in order. You might find a different sequence, for one student might suggest:

When the alarm clock goes off in the morning, I have to get up, eat breakfast, get dressed, and catch a bus before 7:30.

Another way to practice sequencing is to cut apart the panels of a comic strip, asking your students to reassemble them so they make sense. This activity often requires careful attention to visual details as well as to the words quoted.

Look around you. You'll find many commercial products that can provide additional skill practice in following directions and in sequencing.

Silent Reading

It is often suggested that adult new readers sometimes be given material below their reading levels. This practice has many advantages, including building the confidence of new readers as they read right along without stumbling. It also allows for comprehension, not just reading word-by-word or calling words. However, at times you want to challenge new readers, to encourage them to push ahead, to let them know that they are capable of reading and understanding more than they realize.

One tutor, leaving on an extended trip, was trying to prepare his student for more independent work. The tutor looked for material at a slightly higher reading level than usual. The subject matter had to be interesting and sufficiently tantalizing for him to want to read on. She got the *Reader's Digest* version of a story and gave him a copy. He looked at it and immediately said that it looked too difficult.

The tutor suggested that he read the first two pages silently. Afterwards he was to tell what he'd read. Almost immediately he asked the tutor what one word was, since he couldn't sound it out, he didn't know it by sight, and it didn't look like any pattern he'd had. She asked him just to skip it, and read along. She thought he'd get the idea.

Shortly, he asked for help on another word. The tutor again suggested skipping the word. After several attempts to get the words from the tutor, the student shrugged his shoulders and continued reading.

When he looked up, finished, the tutor asked him what he had read. He was excited for he realized that he could comprehend without reading every word and could easily retell the story.

You as the tutor must know when to give reading material below readers' levels and when to challenge them with material beyond their levels. Suggesting high-interest material that challenges learners to stretch is another teaching technique that shouldn't be overlooked.

Reading Out Loud

Don't overlook having your students read aloud even though some are hesitant to do this, embarrassed because they know how awkward they sound. Reading aloud is a goal for many students—perhaps reading passages from the Bible at church, reading reports at a meeting at work, reading to their children. Practice makes perfect, and you should encourage your students to practice reading aloud. There are several suggestions to help students read aloud in Chapter 4 (see pages 77–79).

SUMMARY

Often motivation can be maintained and comprehension enhanced by varying the materials. Games, maps, calendars, letters, tape recorders, and computer-assisted instruction can all be used to reinforce learning. But if your students have not been motivated by any of these suggestions, perhaps their rate of learning can be improved by a more structured approach. In all cases, be patient, be flexible, be creative, and be aware of your students' reactions to the learning and teaching taking place.

Be sure that new learning is firmly based on what your students already know. Don't limit yourself to the suggested motivational materials and activities given in this book. Invent a few of your own!

Volunteer tutors constantly come up with new, creative ways of teaching. Reading is a partnership among tutors, librarians, family, friends, and students. To teach literacy skills successfully you must provide practical, planned instruction using materials that are meaningful to your students. And you must do it in a relaxed, accepting manner.

ASSESSMENT AND LESSON PLANNING

Formal Assessment
Grade Equivalents and Readability Formulas

Informal Assessment
Diagnostic Tests
Portfolios

Other Kinds of Assessment
Observations
Oral Reading
Writing
Seeing/Hearing/Other Problems

Lesson Planning
Lesson Plans
Identifying Appropriate Material
A Typical Lesson Plan
A Lesson for a Low-Level Reader/Writer
Lessons for an Intermediate Reader/Writer

Points to Remember in Planning a Lesson
Lesson Plan Step-by-Step

Summary

LITERACY INSTRUCTION should begin by focusing on each learner's expressed needs at the level of his skills. Instruction will yield assessment information which can then be used to develop lesson plans and/or refine existing plans.

From this point of view, assessment is the close examination of a student's progress toward his or her own goals. But first the tutor must find out what the students already know and where they need help or reinforcement. The evidence of progress is in the collected records and samples of student work. *Assessment* is the process of collecting and reviewing the information. *Evaluation* involves making judgments about the quality of the work. Progress, then, is noted as there is evidence of positive change in the quality of the samples collected.

FORMAL ASSESSMENT

Many adult basic education programs test according to state requirements. If states give funding to an educational program, that program must monitor progress for public accountability. Programs need to identify and evaluate instructional practices and measure student achievement. Standardized assessment tests include the Adult Basic Learning Examination (BEST), CASAS Adult Life Skills, and the Test for Adult Basic Education (TABE). These tests measure student achievement from one level to another. Some give general indication of where students need help, such as "in words in context," "in constructing meaning," "in multiplication using whole numbers." A Pre-Test is usually given when a student enters an adult literacy program, and a Post-Test at a later designated time to show whether progress was made.

Grade Equivalents and Readability Formulas

Much of the material available for both instruction and testing is given a "grade level" difficulty ranking. The grade level is most often determined by the use of one of many readability formulas. Be careful not to rely solely on readability formulas to measure the suitability of a particular title for adult new readers. Readability formulas focus on such things as number of words and syllables, sentence length, and use of word lists. No readability formula measures such key factors as a reader's prior knowledge or interest in the topic. However, if you're unsure of the level of any given material you're reviewing for your student, readability formulas do give an approximate level for you to consider.

Since readability formulas cannot be viewed as entirely trustworthy, it follows that graded materials used in testing can't be viewed as yielding hard and fast grade equivalents for students either. A beginning student who has difficulty with the nonsense language used in many Dr. Seuss books may have greater success with a note she has written (or dictated) to her child's teacher even though the note may contain several multi-syllabic words that can't be sounded out. A student with more proficiency may find reading the driver's manual a challenge but have no trouble with the sports page of the daily newspaper. Some more advanced students may do very well on test items but may find it difficult to read and retell a simple short story. By the same token, of course, many good readers may have to reread the text of legal contracts or insurance policies.

Reading is more than just learning to pronounce words and marking the correct answers. The more experience or prior knowledge students bring to a text on a given topic, the more control they are likely to have over that text. Readers use all the clues available to them: the print on the page (letters, sounds, words); the context of the language in print; their own experience and knowledge of the topic; and their own vocabulary and language proficiencies. Therefore, the more of these clues there are, the less difficult reading becomes. The fewer the clues, the more difficult the reading.

We prefer to look at proficiency in reading as broad ranges of ability rather than as narrow grade levels. For our purposes in this discussion, the following will apply:

Proficiency Range	Traditional Grade Equivalent
Beginning	0 to 1st grade
Early Intermediate	2nd to 3rd grade
Intermediate	4th to 5th grade
Advanced	above 5th grade

Tutors must understand that in spite of grade levels, adults are much more competent than children at the same grade level. Use these grade levels in a respectful way.

INFORMAL ASSESSMENT

For daily or weekly tutoring sessions, you might find more informal, easy-to-do assessments helpful. They can show specific accomplishments and help you plan your lessons. But remember that struggling students are scared of any tests. Be sure to explain that there is no "pass-fail"—it's diagnostic, in that it helps a tutor/teacher find out what a student already knows and where he/she needs help.

To help plan where to start their instruction, tutors and teachers need to know what skills the students already possess and what gaps need to be addressed. If a student has mastered all letter-sound relationships, it's not necessary to teach phonics. However, a student might recognize most of the letter-sound relationships, but not know the sounds of g, h, k, q, and x. It would be helpful for the tutor to know if that student recognizes any sight words, or if so about how many? Does the student understand that English is a patterned language and that certain known patterns help us read new words? Does a student have problems with reversal of letters? What about comprehension? Can problems in comprehension be identified?

Keeping samples of a student's writings, records of that student's background, materials read, and attendance can also show progress.

Diagnostic Tests

There are informal assessments designed to identify and measure students' progress with specific reading and/or writing strategies and skills. However, a majority of these tests were developed for children and are inappropriate for either teenagers or adults. To fill the need for an easily administered tool for adults, Jane Root and I developed *READ: Reading Evaluation—Adult Diagnosis* (rev. 1999 by Hinchman and Shoultz, New Readers Press), which provides for the measurement of the following competencies:

1. Basic sight word recognition.
2. Specific word analysis skills in relation to:
   Names and sounds of letters (consonants)
   Blends (*bl, br*)
   Word patterns (*mat, sat, fat*)
   Reversals (*was* for *saw*)
   Variant vowels (vowel sounds other than the short vowels).
3. Level of reading ability (word recognition in context).
4. Levels of reading and listening comprehension.

Information from *READ* will help you decide which skills need reinforcement and what portion of your lesson should be devoted to each skill. Since the results give approximate levels of reading and listening comprehension, you could also use them as a general guide in developing lessons and selecting materials.

Of course, *READ* is just one of the many measures you can use. Check with your coordinator to find out which measures are used in your program. Whether you use *READ* or other evaluation instruments, you should know that a reading level is a rather nebulous concept. A score used to determine a reading level on any test should be looked at as a rough estimate and not as the definitive answer about a particular student's ability.

Portfolios

Portfolios, folders where individual students' records are kept, add breadth to student assessment. A portfolio houses multiple pieces of information about a student, not just one test score or one information sheet. In addition to personal records, keep samples of your students' work in individual portfolios. A student-centered, multi-measure portfolio assessment might include the following:

- personal information—address, telephone, background
- writing samples
- notes on student's strengths and needs
- list of student's long-term and short-term goals
- record of materials read
- record of student's attendance
- personal word list
- progress reports
- student's self-evaluations
- student's expressed interests and concerns.

At regular intervals—perhaps monthly—tutors and students might agree to review the folders. Together you can review the materials read, read early writing samples and compare them to later writings, and mark off goals attained. This review is a great motivator for students and a practical way for you to keep records.

OTHER KINDS OF ASSESSMENT

Observations

Finding your students' interests and concerns through questions and conversations helps you to identify what materials are best suited for them. Be prepared to share what you enjoy doing before you ask questions about your students' interests. Such sharing can provide the basis for a relaxed give and take conversation. Listen to what your students say, paraphrasing to be sure you understand their feelings, interests and concerns. The Reading/Writing Inventory in the Appendix (see pages 173–175) may help you focus such a discussion with students. Note their interests in their portfolios for future reference.

Oral Reading

You might want to add notes you made as you listened to your students read aloud to portfolios. As students read aloud, listen for patterns and make mental notes of answers to these questions:

- Do they hesitate before each word?
- Do they consistently miscall certain letters or words?
- Do they read word-by-word instead of in phrases?
- Do they read with good intonation, using their voices to denote questions, commands, or dialogue?
- Do they pause at the ends of sentences?
- Do they stop at the ends of paragraphs?
- For words that are miscalled, is the problem one of misreading (*cow* for *could*) or one of seeing one word and calling it a similar word (*house* for *home*)?
- Do students catch themselves when the words they read do not make sense? (Do readers say, "Oh, that doesn't make sense" when they read "I was so sick I cow not eat my supper"?)

Listening for answers to these eight questions as students read will help you plan instruction that addresses students' needs. Also, the answers will give you good information from which to plan instruction in your lessons.

Writing

When viewing student writing, look for patterns. Plan instruction that addresses the needs that show up in the students' writing. Let these questions guide you as you make notes for each student's portfolio:

1. Fluency. How much do students write? Does the text seem to flow?

2. Structure. Does the text have a structure? Does it narrate; describe; give a sequence; go through the process; give examples; list reasons, causes, effects; state a problem and offer a solution? Or does the text seem to ramble on with no apparent sense of organization?

3. Vocabulary. Do students vary use of vocabulary or do they use the same words over and over again in their writing? Do they use vocabulary appropriately? Is the vocabulary concrete (words you can "see"), or do they use vague pronouns and linking verbs *(is, are, was, were)*?

4. Development of Ideas. Do students explain key ideas, using examples or details? Or do they expect the reader to read their minds?

5. Syntax (word order within a sentence). Do all sentences follow the subject and verb pattern, or do the students vary sentence structure with introductory phrases or clauses?

   Are there any irregular placements that English speakers don't generally make (for example, "the doll little" instead of "the little doll" or "to running" instead of "to run")?

6. Mechanics and Usage. Do students have trouble with spelling, subject-verb agreement, pronoun agreement, verb forms, pronoun forms, punctuation, or capitalization? Do students write incomplete sentences (fragments) or run several sentences together with commas or no punctuation?

Seeing/Hearing/Other Problems

Before proceeding with instruction, watch for indications of any difficulties the learners appear to have in vision, hearing, behavior, or learning.

Do students squint, read with one eye covered, tip their heads so that the bridge of the nose obscures the vision in one eye, hold the book too close or too far away, rub their eyes, or complain of eye fatigue? Each of these symptoms suggests a referral to a vision specialist. Many areas have organizations that will provide free glasses.

Must learners look at you to be sure of hearing what you say? Is one side or another favored while listening? Do you have to repeat things often? Do they speak loudly even when there are no other noises to distract the listeners? These symptoms suggest that a hearing screening may be needed.

You may also encounter learners who have other problems that may not be easily identified through casual observation. Such learners may have great difficulty linking the words they see with the words they speak. They may have learning disabilities or difficulties. Chapter 10 deals with such learning problems.

If you encounter a suspected sight, hearing, or other problem, inform your program staff as soon as possible so that appropriate action can be suggested.

LESSON PLANNING

You must now translate learner-centered goals, results of diagnostic tests, and your assessment of each student into objectives for learning. You must now make practical lesson plans that, while flexible, progress in a logical manner toward accomplishment of each learner's goals—first the short-term and eventually the long-term goals. Your lesson planning will follow naturally and will be composed of the following parts:

1. Assessment
2. Instruction
3. Evaluation

Lesson Plans

You know your student's long-term and short-term goals. What are the objectives, the steps to attaining his or her short-term goal? What particular objective do you want your learner to accomplish toward that goal by the end of the lesson?

Some tutors find that writing the goals, objectives, and techniques to be used, and even jotting down what materials to bring, can help them plan individual lessons. Here's one example:

Student's name: John		**Date:** May 23
Long-term Goal: To read the drivers' manual and pass the written test		
Short-term Goal: To read and understand the first chapter in the manual		
Objective	**Techniques**	**Materials**
Read two pages of driver's manual	Student read aloud 2 pages to identify unknown words and check comprehension	Drivers' manual
Learn unknown words on 2 pages	Sight words, phonics, patterned words	Tutor, word cards
Identify meanings of 3 road signs by shape	Sight words, comprehension	road signs

Identifying Appropriate Material

Student interest is of primary concern in planning lessons. It is important to involve students when selecting books and other materials that will be used either for instruction or for recreational reading.

Bring several books to class or take your students to the library. Encourage them to look for books of interest. Point out the various things to look for when selecting a book. Ask the students what the cover tells. Ask them to look at the chapter headings, the table of contents, and the introduction. Have them look at the pictures or illustrations and skim the book, reading random sentences and paragraphs. If you are working with a small group of learners, you may want to have them work in pairs, examining and discussing which book to choose.

Ask your students to choose among several books you think will be of interest. Have each student read a few paragraphs silently. If any student thinks a passage is too difficult, have him or her look at other books until an appropriate book is found.

A Typical Lesson Plan

A simple Lesson Plan form in the Appendix (see page 176) can be photocopied. It includes name, date, student's goals, and a place to jot down the sequence of your lesson, including what you actually completed today and what you want to include in the next lesson.

Review homework • If you've given a home assignment and your student has worked perhaps hours to do it, it's only courteous to collect it and review it together or take it home and return it to your student with comments. Reviewing and evaluating homework together demonstrates to students that working on their own is a vital part of learning to read and write.

Review previous lesson • Few of us can master a new skill or a new task with only one explanation or trial. Your lessons contain many concepts new to your students that must be reviewed and practiced many times before they are learned thoroughly. Confidence is built as mastery is completed.

Don't be misled into thinking that all review is boring to your students. Although it may seem repetitious to you, remember that this is new material to your students. You may want to vary the way you review, but be assured that review cements skills and concepts in the minds of students.

New work or work in progress • This is the heart of each lesson, including the actual materials and techniques that you plan to use that particular day. Be sure the skills you are teaching are broken into steps small enough to be thoroughly mastered and reinforced in a relatively short time.

Adjust your plan as you go along. Each lesson provides the basis for planning future lessons. Experience stories give insights to learner interests; reading and writing activities reveal strengths and shortcomings in word analysis and comprehension; writing samples reveal strengths and indicate needs for instruction in spelling, punctuation, grammar usage, and vocabulary.

Remember that mastery in one lesson does not guarantee long-range mastery. You'll be reviewing some material in the same session in which you'll be introducing new concepts. If, despite repeated exposure and simplified objectives, little mastery seems to have been attained, drop the activity and return to it later when it will seem new again, and may seem more relevant to the student.

Reinforcing Activities • Include in your lesson everyday activities to reinforce the lessons learned. For example, you can work with games, maps, calendars, letters, recordings, notes, computers, newspapers, and puzzles, as described in Chapter 7.

Homework • Homework assignments should be planned with the students and should be part of every lesson. Your students may not respond to this easily, so try to make homework interesting and appropriate, explaining why it is important. Reading and writing achievements will often come slowly if they must be acquired with only two or three hours a week of involvement. Reading and writing must be exercised to be acquired or maintained. No one learns to read or write without practice, and it is the learner who must do the practicing. Don't even imply that reading and writing can be taught during the lesson time alone. You and your student may have signed a written agreement (see Appendix, page 196), where he or she agreed to do perhaps ten minutes of practice or homework each day.

Make it easy to take work home. You could write short homework assignments, so your students could even work on homework during coffee breaks. Learners could read for ten minutes, keeping a record of what they've read and sharing it with you at the next meeting.

Home practice will vary depending on the needs and abilities of the students as well as the work done at a particular session and the time students have to commit. Here are some possible activities:

- Reread Language Experience stories and word cards.
- Practice word cards from personal word lists.
- Review letter-sound relationships learned in the last lesson, perhaps circling those letters on a newspaper page.
- Take a copy of writing home to reread or to rewrite.
- Read a page or a chapter from a library book every night.
- Read the words on a menu from a local restaurant.
- Read for ten minutes every day and keep a record of what is read.
- Write in a journal three or four times a week, even if each writing consists of just a sentence or two.
- Follow a recipe to prepare some kind of food.
- Make a list of things to do or items to buy at a store.
- Play a word game with a family member.
- Fill out a sample application for a library card or bank account.
- Write a message on a postcard and mail it to a friend.
- Work on the computer at the library.
- Complete a workbook assignment.
- Listen to a recorded reading.

The possibilities are limited only by your own imagination and that of your students. To become a better reader and writer requires frequent reading and writing. Two sessions a week will not provide sufficient practice time for meaningful progress to take place. Therefore, it is imperative that students understand that between-lesson practice is crucial to learning to read and write. But don't be surprised if your student does no or little homework. Sometimes home and work responsibilities take precedence. Both you and your students must understand that with no or little home practice, progress will necessarily be slower.

Reading for Pleasure • As you try hard to teach your students all the skills involved in reading, be sure to let them know that reading is fun. Use the last five or ten minutes of your lesson to read aloud to your students. You could read a short article on a sport your students enjoy, a simple mystery continued from lesson to lesson, or an inspirational story.

You could record any of these readings for the learners to review at home, thus extending the lesson time. Planning a final few minutes of reading aloud emphasizes that reading can be fun.

Student's Comments • At the end of each lesson, discuss with your students their feelings about the lesson. Find out if there is anything they'd like to do more of or anything they didn't like. Decide together what the objectives of the next lesson will be. Get their ideas for what they'd like to work on next. Listening to and using your students' ideas strengthens their motivation by showing them that their ideas are important.

Tutor's Notes • After each lesson, write your own notes about your students' progress on the day's lesson plan. While your students' work is fresh in your mind, write your plans for the next lesson, basing the objectives on your students' performance, interests, and needs.

Some tutors have limited time for lesson planning. After they have created an initial lesson plan, they can "continuous plan" by using a loose leaf or spiral notebook, putting the initial information on the left side of the first page, and moving on to the next column for the next lesson (see Appendix, page 177). You can quickly see what is needed for the next lesson and continue planning page after page.

A Lesson for a Low-Level Reader/Writer

Mark is a learner in a small group of fathers organized around the topic of reading to children. His long-range goal is to get a high school diploma. His short-range goals are to read children's books to his children and to help them with their homework. Mark has little confidence in his reading and no confidence in his writing ability. He reads at a lower level than any other father in the small group and has recently begun one-to-one tutoring in addition to the small group.

In planning Mark's one-to-one instruction, his tutor works closely with the small group tutor, who keeps records of which books the small group has chosen. The majority of instruction in Mark's one-to-one lessons is directly related to the particular book the group is reading at the time. These lessons have included assisted reading and work on comprehension in addition to word attack skills.

In his second tutoring session, Mark was excited about reading a child's book. He worked with his tutor in an assisted-reading situation. Immediately after reading the book, the tutor asked, "What did you like about that book?" This question sparked a lively discussion.

Mark made his own word cards from five words in the book, but he also wanted to make word cards of his children's names. He and the tutor worked on word patterns formed from *look* (a word that appeared several times in the text of the child's story) and *book,* using the list in the Appendix (see page 189) to get other patterned words (*cook, hook, took*).

Mark and his tutor decided that a notebook in which Mark would keep a summary of the plots from the various children's books would be a help when the family went to the library. However, when the tutor suggested that Mark write a few sentences about the book they had just read, he balked. "I can't write," he said. The tutor assessed the situation.

"We've talked about the book. You like it because . . ." and the tutor recounted what Mark had said.

"I just can't write," Mark repeated.

"Mark, if you could write anything, what would it be?" asked the tutor.

"I think I'd like to write a letter to my mom about the kids," Mark replied.

Mark, like many other students, was frightened of writing. Because the tutor found what Mark wanted to write, they had a base for starting the actual writing.

The tutor found that all the language components—listening, speaking, reading, and writing—could easily be included in each lesson. Their discussions involved listening and speaking, and with the tutor's help, Mark decided he wanted to work on specific projects in both reading and writing.

Lessons for an Intermediate Reader/Writer

Sarah is a single parent with two children, ages 6 and 8. Now 26 years old, she dropped out of school when she was 16, having completed 8th grade. Sarah has worked in several jobs, and is now working in a small office where she answers the phone and does simple filing. She's dependable and well liked, and has been asked to take on more responsibilities, which would mean an increase in pay. But she's had to decline because she lacks skills in writing, in using the computer, and in reading the material her company sends out.

Sarah's long-term goal is to get that upgraded job, but she also wants to be able to help her children in their school work. She doesn't want them to be limited in their careers as she has been.

Testing showed that Sarah is at the Intermediate level in reading and writing (equivalent to the 5th grade), that she can decode words, can read simple material fairly well, and can comprehend most of what she can read. However, her oral reading is hesitant, mostly word-by-word, for she has little confidence in herself. Her handwriting isn't always legible, and she says she hates to write anything. She knows she must learn to write better and she's willing to try—but she doesn't know how to start.

Sarah and her tutor discussed what short-term goals would move her toward that new job. Together they decided to work on Sarah's writing skills, to start using a computer even if she had to use the "hunt and peck" system at first, and to get copies of her company's reading material. To help her children, they decided to get copies of the children's homework so Sarah could do the homework with the children.

They started with Language Experience—Sarah was eager to talk, to share stories of her children. At first the tutor let Sarah dictate, and the tutor wrote out the stories. Both were surprised when Sarah decided to write up stories that she had told her children as they were growing up—stories of "good guys" and "bad guys," of how the "good guys" always helped others and won in the long run.

They met at a local library where computers were available, and Sarah couldn't wait to put her stories on the computer. She was ashamed of her poor handwriting and loved seeing the stories in print. She took them home to read to her children.

Sarah brought in her company's promotional material. As part of each lesson, they read it together, and Sarah explained its meaning. She knew the company's material and its policies, but she had never tried to really read its materials. The more she read, the more confident she became, and after four months, she talked to her boss, saying she thought she was ready for added responsibilities.

Sarah and her tutor continued their lessons with more writing, giving opportunities for Sarah to learn about outlining (mapping), spelling, punctuation, and proper grammar. Sarah brought in more advanced reading materials from her company, focusing on comprehension and critical thinking (she brought some new ideas to the company). Her children brought their mother's stories to class and read them to their friends. They were SO proud of their mother.

Sarah added a new goal—she wanted to get her GED diploma.

POINTS TO REMEMBER IN PLANNING A LESSON

1. **Assess and Review** • As you plan for the next lesson, remember to assess and review your notes from the current lesson plan.

2. **Overplan** • It is better to have too much planned than not enough. The excess goes over into the next lesson, or you may want to skip some planned activities in favor of others.

3. **Overteach** • When your students can retain something for a period of at least three lessons, you may assume that it is learned. Don't panic when what you thought was learned seems to have been forgotten. Re-learning will come faster than the original learning.

4. **Be Flexible** • Many a good lesson on paper fails to work well because a learner is upset, circumstances intervene, or some other part of your plan took longer than you had anticipated.

5. **Be Positive** • Encourage your students, but be honest. Guarantee some success with every lesson.

6. **Be Efficient** • Make your plans carefully. It is the best way to assure that you will be relaxed yet alert to the needs of your students. Note successes as well as needs on the lesson plan during lessons.

Lesson Plan Step-by-Step

With the students' goals identified, here's a checklist to use when making a lesson plan. The sample lesson plan templates in the Appendix (see pages 176–177) can be photocopied for your use.

1. Review homework.
2. Review previous lesson.
3. Do new work or work in progress.
4. Plan reinforcing activities.
5. Assign homework.
6. Read for pleasure.
7. Ask students for comments.
8. Write your own notes.

SUMMARY

Careful planning and common sense are a good combination. As you gain experience, you will learn to use a variety of techniques, shifting from one to another easily as the occasion demands. You will be able to use them with both the materials you and your students develop and with published material. On-the-spot intervention requires a skilled tutor who can assess and adapt immediately. That comes with practice.

Creativity is not the privilege only of the professional. Volunteers constantly come up with new and better ways of teaching. To teach literacy successfully you must provide skilled instruction using materials that are meaningful to your students. And you must do it in a relaxed and accepting environment.

INTERVIEWS, FIRST MEETINGS, AND TUTOR-STUDENT MATCH

Student Interviews

First Meetings With Students
  What to Bring
  Introductions
  Rules, Roles, Responsibilities
  Student/Tutor Agreement
  An Example of a First Meeting

Ongoing Meetings

Summary

YOU'VE HAD YOUR BASIC LITERACY TRAINING. You've practiced the techniques suggested in *Tutor*. You've been assigned a student, and you're ready for the next step. But you wonder a bit about how your student was prepared for this first meeting. In this chapter we'll discuss student interviews and give suggestions for those most important first meetings with your students. We'll also consider the roles you and your students will play as you continue your work together.

STUDENT INTERVIEWS

Each tutoring program has its own particular guidelines for interviewing students and for matching them with tutors. Information collected during an initial intake interview includes name, address, telephone number, age, number of years of schooling, marital status, employment, as well as information on when and where a potential student can meet. Asking students to write their own names and addresses gives initial evidence of writing ability.

The interviewer will also note why students want to improve their reading and writing proficiencies and will record their interests, needs, and goals. The program office uses this data to help select compatible tutors for students and to give tutors background information on their students. Other forms allow the interviewer to find out more about students' interests, goals, and current reading and writing habits.

The interview is usually conducted by the program's matcher or by some other person whose role is to interview prospective learners and, usually, to give a standardized test (see Chapter 8—Assessment). What is learned from this interview and test is given to the tutor prior to meeting with the student or small group. This program interview is an individual interview, even if the student eventually goes into a small group or into a classroom situation.

FIRST MEETINGS WITH STUDENTS

First meetings are as significant for the students as for the tutors. First impressions are always important. While you're anxious to meet your students, know that your students will be looking you over too, deciding if they want to continue this new adventure into learning more of reading and writing. The meeting should be positive and non-threatening, a time to encourage your students by showing your interest and concern for them.

You have read this book; you have discussed and practiced approaches to and techniques for tutoring; you have reviewed various case histories and have seen samples of student writing; you may have met and talked with some students during your training. You have been assigned your student(s) and have some background information based on an intake interview. Now what? Your first lesson starts before you get to the tutoring site. Your first session starts with preparation.

Before the first session, review all the information about your students that your program has given you. You should have the results of the program's intake interview and possibly the results of a state required standardized test to help you prepare for your first meeting with the learners. You will know basic information about each student: name, age, and educational background. You will have an inkling of each student's interests and a general feel for individual reading ability.

You were given your students' telephone numbers. Call your students to check on the time and place for the first session, making sure your students know how to get there. You may have found space in a library, a bank's public meeting room, a community room at a mall, a church, or a union hall. Perhaps your program has a recommended list of available sites. In any case, a good place is a neutral one.

What to Bring

What should you bring to a first lesson? Tutors can keep all their teaching materials in a bag, a briefcase, or a large folder. You might want to include

1. each student's name, address, phone number, and educational information;

2. name tag for yourself and students, written in large manuscript letters (if working with a small group or in a classroom setting);

3. notebook, paper, and pens or pencils;

4. a copy of *Tutor*;

5. *READ Test* or other diagnostic or informal assessment;

6. notebook or folder for your records;

7. portfolios (folders) for your copy of each student's writing samples and other portfolio information;

8. student portfolios or folders for storing their own writing;

9. real-life reading material of high interest to your learners;

10. low-level, high-interest books from the library;

11. 3" x 5" cards;

12. beginners' dictionary;

13. a calendar for each student, to keep dates for lessons and appointments;

14. blank Student/Tutor Agreement (see Appendix, page 196);

15. motivational material to read to your student;

16. your lesson plan;

17. a standing easel/chalkboard/whiteboard (optional but especially helpful for small groups or classrooms).

Introductions

It's good practice to be at your session site before the students arrive. In a one-to-one situation, sit next to the learner. A round table is desirable for a group meeting, but if you must use a rectangular table, avoid sitting at the head. This physical arrangement plays down traditional teacher-student roles and cues the learners that this is a team effort, fostering a "we're all in this together" spirit.

If it's a small group or a class, give each student a name tag with the name written in big manuscript letters. Wear a tag with your name clearly visible too. Introduce yourself, and suggest that students introduce themselves. Give your own name, occupation, family status, hobbies, and perhaps your reason for being there. Your own introduction will guide learners as to what is expected of them.

Remind the students that the goal of the program is to improve reading and writing rather than to learn to read. Only a small percentage of the adult population is totally illiterate. The more frequent need lies with people who can read some words, but who cannot read well and, more importantly, cannot understand what they read.

During this first meeting, you will be able to go into greater depth or ask clarification questions about information collected in the program's interview. Both you and your students will be using this information to set goals and plan the kinds of materials and topics to use during lessons. However, be sensitive about probing unnecessarily into a student's personal background.

Explain what types of exercises might be included in a lesson. Encourage your students to bring any reading material they find difficult and would like to be able to read, such as school notices, doctor bills, or newspapers. Suggest that each student bring a folder or notebook for class work (unless you plan to furnish them).

The tutor-student first meeting should accomplish the following objectives:

1. Get to know each other and agree on time and place for lessons.
2. Establish rapport and encourage participation.
3. Discuss rules, roles, and responsibilities.
4. Start discussion of long-term and short-term goals.
5. Help students articulate their specific interests and concerns.
6. Plan the course of instruction together.

Early assessment should include:

1. Interview by program director, including a standardized test
2. Tutor/student early meeting, asking student to read aloud
3. Tutor giving a diagnostic test to identify word recognition skills and listening/reading comprehension (informal reading inventory)

Rules, Roles, Responsibilities

Rules • Discussing the ground rules for the sessions presents you with your first opportunity to involve students in making significant decisions. The participants will see that individual members' needs and preferences are being considered and that the democratic process is at work.

Explain that there must be a few ground rules. Suggest some—such as being on time or calling when you cannot attend—and solicit others. Encourage discussion through questioning and be careful not to suggest all the rules. Write down the rules and give the students copies.

With a small group or a class, you might include such things as being patient with others who may be having trouble keeping up, listening to the suggestions and questions of others, making positive comments or questions, not having to read aloud unless individuals want to, allowing others to finish before speaking, and completing assignments for home practice. It will be each member's responsibility to include others in discussions as well as not to monopolize discussions. In both a one-to-one and small group format, you could start the discussion with your expectation that students will make at least one positive remark about their own reading or writing and that any reading to be done aloud can be done silently first.

Most meeting places do not allow smoking, but you might want to let your students know that there will be no smoking during lessons. While many one-to-one sessions last only one hour, if yours is a two-hour session, you might want to include a ten-minute break.

The Tutor's Roles and Responsibilities • Keeping the session on track may involve constantly clarifying both tutor and learner roles. In a one-to-one learning partnership, there are only the two of you. In a typical small group situation, there will probably be a tutor and three-to-five learners, for a total small group size of four-to-six members. In a classroom setting there will be even more participants. In any situation, you and the learners must define the roles of participants to be sure that expectations can be set and met.

As a tutor you have differing and sometimes changing roles in a collaborative reading and writing situation: housekeeper, facilitator, leader, instructor. As housekeeper, you set the times and dates, secure and confirm a site, and notify the learners if there are changes. As facilitator, you assume the roles of leader, counselor, and negotiator, even in a one-to-one situation. These same responsibilities are important in a group setting when and if the group faces conflict and frustration. As tutor, you can help strengthen the group as a team.

You will find yourself taking an active role as leader early in the development of the tutoring relationship. Because this new learning situation may make some students uncomfortable, they need to know that someone is in charge. Your role will change during the life of the learning partnership as the students become more self confident and independent, taking more active roles. It is also your job to disband the one-to-one pair or small group when the time comes.

Your most important job is that of instructor. You will decide on the support materials, continue to help clarify objectives during the sessions, and develop lesson plans as your assessment of learners' progress evolves. Your commitment includes not only taking the necessary training, but also

- mastering the tutoring techniques;
- teaching at least one student at least two hours a week for a minimum of fifty hours a year;
- keeping records of each student's progress and discussing them with each student as well as with your program coordinator. You might set aside ten or fifteen minutes every month to review each learner's goals and his or her portfolio, reviewing accomplishments together;
- planning lessons based on your students' goals, assessment, interests, strengths, and needs, and having appropriate materials available;
- reporting your students' goal achievements, improvement in reading and writing, interest changes, hours of instruction, and differences in relationships within the family, the workplace, and the community, to your program coordinator.

As time passes, you will probably note that the students will become more productive, show more responsibility for their learning, and become more accepting of differences. As these things happen, your role as the authority figure will lessen. You set the tone of flexibility and relaxed acceptance.

The Students' Roles and Responsibilities • It's important that students make a commitment for a definite period of time. This allows students to plan and arrange their schedules and to take additional classes if the need arises. Encourage your students to commit to learning as a lifelong activity.

Real learning requires active participation. A major part of each student's responsibility is to agree to some home practice. Discuss and plan with the student the amount of time and the kind of homework activities that are appropriate.

In general, you can expect learners to gradually assume responsibility for some of their own learning. They should

- attend sessions regularly and on time;
- call the tutor if unable to attend a session;
- participate in making ground rules;
- help plan individual (and group) goals;
- help design activities or strategies to achieve identified goals;
- participate in those activities, making positive comments and asking clarifying questions;
- show respect for each other's rights and opinions;
- agree to confidentiality;
- do agreed upon homework assignments.

Student/Tutor Agreement

Questions come up, such as "How long should I work with my new learner?" "I think that my learner should move to a new learning experience, but how shall I tell him?" "How can I get my student to do homework?" One way to address these issues is to propose an agreement with students that would be in effect for a specific period of time and be subject to renewal if the circumstances warrant.

Perhaps you will discover that a student has serious problems and that learning to read and write will necessitate professional help. When the contract period has passed, a new contract might be drawn up giving very specific and limited goals. You might say to your student: "During the next four weeks, I think you can learn forty important words. When you learn these new words, you will be much better off than you were before, and then we'll decide if we should continue lessons." Write up the agreement. In this way you can teach some survival skills and begin to prepare for termination.

Suppose a student has been delinquent in attending lessons. You both review the agreement at the end of the designated period, and you can say very frankly, "Well, there were a good many times you missed your lesson. I think you've got so many other things you're concerned about that learning to read and write better isn't the highest thing on your list right now. Perhaps later on you'll be ready for more lessons."

When you, as a tutor, are certain that your student has truly tried, but is just not learning, be honest about it. You might say, "You know, reading is really tough and all of us are made differently. There's lots about reading that we just don't know. Let's go to the program coordinator to see if we can find you some more help." This makes it possible for both learner and tutor to break off their relationship with some measure of dignity.

The agreement system might well provide an "out" for the learner who isn't learning but who hesitates to make the break. If the contract expires within a specific time, there is no danger of either the learner or the tutor being trapped in a fruitless situation.

On the other hand, if the learner has made progress, you can say at the end of the agreement period, "Look at all you've learned. Now that you know how to learn, you can learn even more. So, let's discuss our agreement for the next ten weeks."

Perhaps your student feels ready to move on from a one-to-one teaching situation to a small group or even a classroom setting.

A sample Student/Tutor Agreement form is in the Appendix (see page 196). Give a signed copy to your student and keep one for yourself.

An Example of a First Meeting

Jo Smith came to a local literacy program, saying she wanted to get her high school diploma. The intake interviewer found that Jo had attended seven years of school before dropping out because she "couldn't read words." Turning to one of the word lists in the back of *Tutor*, the interviewer asked Jo to read a few words. Jo attempted three or four words, miscalling them all. Based on the discussion with Jo and further assessment, the interviewer knew Jo was a very beginning student.

The intake interviewer matched Jo with a tutor to whom this information was given. The tutor called Jo to set a time for a "get acquainted" session or first meeting. Keeping in mind the purposes of that first meeting, the tutor set about to learn more about her student: to get an idea of the student's strengths and needs, to come up with more realistic goals they could use when planning their tutoring sessions together.

In the following conversation, notice that the tutor helped Jo articulate some more easily achievable short-term goals:

Tutor: I see you'd like to work on your high school diploma. A high school diploma is a wonderful goal, but it may take quite a while. If you could tell me why you'd like to earn your diploma, maybe we could set some short-term goals. Why would you like to earn your high school diploma?

Jo: So I can do better on my job and read to my children.

Tutor: What do you need to read at work?

Jo: Well, I want to come to work through the front door. I can't tell which door is mine because I can't read the sign that tells which is the Morgan Dining Hall.

As they continued to talk, the tutor found that for the past few years Jo had used the back door to go to her job in a cafeteria, located in the basement of one in a row of several buildings which all looked alike. She was petrified to go to the front of this row of buildings in the fear that she could not read the sign directing people to the "Morgan Dining Hall" and would be left to wander aimlessly around the area.

Once at work, she was constantly humiliated as patrons ordered "whole wheat," "lite wheat," "white," and "lite white." She could only identify bread by the color, so if she chose the wrong one, she was met by jabs like, "I said lite white. Can't you read?"

The conversation further revealed that Jo had two small children and she wanted to be able to read to them

The tutor was able to make the following suggestions:

Tutor: Jo, we'll make sure you get help as you start work on your high school diploma. Right now, though, I hear you say that you've got three other important goals. You want to read the sign "Morgan Dining Hall," read the labels at your work station, and read to your children.

Jo: That's right. I didn't know you'd help me with those things. I thought you'd only help me go to school.

Tutor: Of course we'll help you with those things. And remember, any reading and writing you do now will eventually help you when it comes time to work on your high school diploma.

The tutor asked Jo if she'd like to write the goals in her notebook. Jo declined, so the tutor wrote them. Remembering the theme of immediate relevance, and since reading "Morgan Dining Hall" was not an overwhelming task, the tutor proceeded with a short lesson.

The tutor and Jo made three word cards: "Morgan," "Dining," and "Hall." Writing, in this case, was not even in sentence form. The tutor wrote each word in manuscript on a sheet of paper, and Jo copied them on 3" x 5" index cards.

From her three word cards, Jo was taught to read "Morgan Dining Hall." The *Hall* part was easy, because she knew the word *all*. She knew the sound of *h* and thus fairly quickly mastered *hall*.

"Dining" was next. She could read *-ing*. *Di-* looks like it sounds, especially if the *i* says its name. Next, the *n* was added to *-ing*. Then, she read *di-ning*.

"Morgan" could have been more difficult to teach, but the tutor didn't let it seem difficult. Jo knew that McDonald's started with *M* (the *M* of the golden arches is great to use with low-level readers). She knew the sound of /*m*/ for *McDonald's* and for *Morgan*.

Notice what the tutor did in this first meeting. She listened to the learner's goals and asked clarification questions. While focusing the student on setting and meeting more immediate short-term goals and needs, the tutor still affirmed the student's long-term goals. She provided concrete information about the program and what it could do. Finally, the tutor helped the student experience immediate and relevant success, reading the sign which would help her identify her workplace.

As you probably realize, students often have difficulty stating a specific short-term or more easily realized goal. Note the long-range goals, but concentrate on the short-range goals that can be accomplished much more quickly. In this way, students will feel the sense of satisfaction needed to keep motivation alive. In this example, the tutor focused on a short-range goal articulated by the student. Through the tutor's asking, not telling, the focus for the learner-centered instruction surfaced quickly. By giving the *READ* test at a subsequent meeting, the tutor was able to identify Jo's specific needs in word identification as well as in listening and reading comprehension.

ONGOING MEETINGS

At your first meeting, you and your students probably discussed and identified long-term goals, but you may not have settled on specific short-term goals. If not, identify short-term goals. (See Chapter 6, Identifying and Setting Goals.) Refer to your assessments and diagnostic tests. They will give you the pattern for your lesson plans. (See Chapter 8, Assessment and Lesson Planning.)

There are no hard and fast rules, but one-to-one teams usually meet at least twice a week for at least an hour per session. Experience has shown that for small groups, two sessions per week, each of two hours' duration, is an effective pattern. After several weeks of following the initial schedule, together you can evaluate its appropriateness. You can always change the schedule.

You are responsible for following or adapting your daily lesson plan and for completing each lesson. It could include any of the reading and writing techniques you have learned as well as games and reinforcing strategies.

As your lessons progress, you will be assessing your students' performance levels in reading and writing as well as their self-confidence. Noting where your students start gives you a baseline for showing improvement.

Don't forget to evaluate with your students what each liked about the session; then decide on the home practice assignment. Remind them of the ground rules you set together for attendance, punctuality, and notifying each other if tutoring appointments cannot be kept.

End the session by reading an inspiring or humorous selection to your students. Some tutors have found that a "continued next session" mystery keeps the students coming back for more.

Don't forget to include your own homework assignments: review, record, make the next lesson plan, and get required materials.

SUMMARY

Once tutors and students are matched and have met, the learning and sharing begin. The Learner Profile (see pages 149–150) is provided to help you focus on specific needs of individual students. After a lesson or two, you may want to use this as a checklist showing where you can find targeted instruction to meet a student's identified needs. Having identified the students' goals, you can turn to your well-planned lessons as the basis for success. Keep in mind that tutors must be willing to adapt their best laid plans to students' often changing needs. Plan ahead, but be prepared to change and adapt. Exciting and challenging days are ahead for both tutors and students.

LEARNING DISABILITIES AND LEARNING DIFFERENCES

With Corinne R. Smith, Ph.D., Syracuse University

RESEARCH AND EXPERIENCE SUGGEST that a sizeable percentage of adults who have reading problems have learning disabilities, or at least have learning differences. Students who have learning disabilities are "unexpected underachievers." This means that learning to read is an unusual struggle in comparison to their other skills. Most of these students have average or above average intelligence. The techniques suggested throughout this book provide well-accepted ways to help learners who have reading problems. The techniques can be adapted to help tutors and students focus on the specific needs of those for whom learning to read is an incredible challenge. Tutors and teachers can modify their lessons to help struggling students find success.

If you've worked with adults for longer than a year to improve their reading and writing skills, and there has been little or no progress, this chapter will assist you. A first suggestion is to check for visual or hearing problems. Do your students put the book too close to their eyes, squint, or put their heads on the desk when reading? Do they complain of headaches when you're working together? Do they turn one ear to you when listening? Your program coordinator can direct them to appropriate places for help.

Some students complain that they have difficulty focusing on words because the words seem to jump around on the page. They tell us that putting a colored overlay over the print seems to reduce the jumping. Although there is no definitive research on this, it can't hurt to try out different color overlays. If the print is more comfortable to read, why not? After all, some of us prefer taking notes on yellow paper rather than white paper, so you might want to experiment with color for your students, too.

Children who have learning difficulties grow up to be adults with learning difficulties, and it's these adults who often are our students. Because these students need individual help, one-to-one sessions seem to have more successful results than work in small groups or in classroom settings. Like the strategies discussed throughout this book, the techniques suggested in this chapter can be adapted for use individually, in small groups, and in classrooms.

MORE ABOUT LEARNING DISABILITIES AND LEARNING DIFFERENCES

Only teams of professionals specializing in learning disabilities are qualified to legally diagnose learning disabilities. As tutors and teachers, however, we can look for signs of learning differences, so that we can adapt our instruction accordingly.

The same issues that affect the academic learning of a person with learning disabilities can also create problematic social issues. Your job as a tutor is to be mainly concerned with helping in the educational area by addressing difficulties with reading, writing, spelling, and math. However, in this chapter we also make you aware of some of the social issues affecting your students.

With respect to individuals with learning disabilities, you may hear terms like *dyslexia, dysgraphia,* and *dyscalculia.* These are medical terms describing any type of brain related reading, writing, and math difficulties. Our brains are complex organs, with one part, the cerebral cortex, controlling all conscious activity. It is in the cerebral cortex that thinking and learning take place. The cerebral cortex is divided into two hemispheres, left and right. These two parts of the brain need to cooperate for us to learn to read, spell, write, and do math. One hemisphere helps us to pay attention to letter sounds so that we can sound out words. This half also helps us to understand reading material, especially focusing on details. The other hemisphere helps us learn to read words by sight, and helps us understand main ideas. Poor learners seem to overuse one or the other cerebral hemisphere with one part stronger than the other.

It's helpful for you, the teacher, to understand that many students with reading challenges struggle in four basic areas: visual (trouble recognizing what words should look like), auditory/language (trouble recognizing individual sounds in words or trouble comprehending the meaning of words and sentences), attention (trouble getting meaning because of a lack of focus), and motor (trouble with eye-hand coordination and, therefore, writing). There are ways that you can help in these areas, discussed later in this chapter under "Targeted Instruction."

Students with learning difficulties are often frustrated, for they do not understand why they are having such problems. As children they may have been put in special education classes, and may have been called dumb, stupid, and lazy. One of our jobs, as tutors and teachers, is to assure these students that they are not dumb, stupid, or lazy. Yes, they do have learning challenges, and they do have different ways of learning. Understanding that you can help them adds to their self confidence, and encourages them to continue to work toward their goals.

Here's a little exercise that might help you understand some of the frustrations that those with learning difficulties feel. It's a simple sentence, but if you have only two learning problems—confusing *b, d, p, q* and a reversal problem (confusing *saw* for *was,* or *pit* for *tip*)—this is how that sentence might look to you. You can see why this takes more time to read.

Boppy saw a haqqy doy when he saw qlaying with his bog.

How long did it take you to realize that the sentence actually said:

Bobby was a happy boy when he was playing with his dog.

Other people are so reflective that they don't see what's right in front of them. How many "f"s are in the following example?

FINISHED FILES ARE THE RESULT OF
YEARS OF SCIENTIFIC STUDY COMBINED
WITH THE YEARS OF EXPERIENCE.

Read aloud the following few words:

A
BIRD
IN THE
THE BUSH

If you found less than six "f"s in the first example, and didn't see the double "the" in the second example, you're with the majority of people.

For those with extraordinary learning challenges, these types of misperceptions occur many times a day. Your patience and encouragement can make the difference between continuing to try and giving up.

IDENTIFYING THOSE WITH LEARNING DIFFERENCES— WHAT TO LOOK FOR

Many programs use one of several instruments to screen learners for *possible* learning disabilities. If the screening indicates the possibility of a learning disability, the student—if he or she chooses to do so—may go to a qualified professional who administers specific tests and interviews the person to determine if a diagnosis of a learning disability is warranted and what kind of disability is present.

What should you look for when you suspect your student has a learning disability? No two students have the same problems, but there are patterns that are common to poor learners and struggling students. If there is a history of reading difficulties in your student's family, this should be noted. By finding out what was helpful in teaching these family members to read, you may happen on a wonderful method to use with your student as well. Most important, we suggest that you check the characteristics listed below, and by administering the *READ* diagnostic test and carefully observing the students' reading patterns, find out what problems affect your students who struggle. Here are some characteristics to look for. You might want to use the Learner Profile sheet (see pages 149–150) to help you focus on your student's specific needs.

Difficulty Focusing

Most of us can do two or more tasks at one time, multi-tasking. We can drive and talk; we can listen to a lecture and take notes. Those with learning difficulties have trouble concentrating on the one task at hand; they have less capacity to maintain attention. Their focus is also influenced by their discomfort when starting a new lesson or a new topic, and by concern about making errors and looking foolish. They are easily distracted by surrounding noises or activities. They prefer to review what they already know.

Longer Time to Process Information

It takes students with learning difficulties longer to process new information. It may take as much as three times the expected time to even read a word they know. They are slow to become fully aware of what they are hearing or seeing and are, therefore, slow in doing any assigned work. They make more mistakes when pressed to hurry.

Memory Difficulties

Many of us have trouble retrieving a name of someone we know well, or forget what we were just about to do or say. (Have you ever walked into a room, then wondered why you were there? You had to stop and think just a moment to retrieve that message from your brain.) Those with learning difficulties may have trouble accessing stored information, and, therefore, have trouble retrieving it.

Many students with learning problems can't retain information from one lesson to the next. When given an assignment one day, they have trouble remembering what was assigned. They have poor retention of new letter-sounds and of new vocabulary words. When read to, they often understand what was read at the time, but have problems recalling it or paraphrasing it a short time later. Too, they often forget appointments. Most often the memory problem is due to the fact that the material was not learned deeply enough to even get stored away in memory. If it isn't stored, of course it won't be remembered.

Reading Difficulties

What they read often doesn't make sense to those with learning difficulties because they struggle so to read the words that they can't concentrate on the message. Many recall a childhood history of problems with reading and spelling. They often complain of headaches and/or extreme fatigue from reading, saying they prefer active sports to reading for pleasure. These struggling readers now realize that the ability to read with comprehension could be important, and might help them solve problems in their daily lives.

Decoding Words • There are often problems decoding words, even though individual sounds may be known. Students may confuse *b* and *d*, *p* and *q*, especially if Roman letters are new to them. Others have difficulty focusing on the specific sounds in a word. (Many are confused if asked whether there is an *"n"* sound in *consider*, for example, or what sound should you write down second in *scratch?*) These students may have problems identifying differences between similar sounds (e.g., the short *"i"* and the short *"e"* as in *"pit"* and *"pet"*) and learning which vowel goes with which sound. It is very confusing when one letter can be pronounced so many different ways, or when one sound can be written in so many ways (*f, gh, ph*). Some students are actually "tone deaf" to sounds that they have not heard in their native languages. Others have trouble blending sounds or hearing individual syllables of a word, even breaking down multi-syllabic words into smaller units. Some don't seem to understand rules of phonics and cannot apply them. Often they are focusing so hard on decoding or on word recognition that what they are reading has little meaning for them.

Reversals • Some students have sound sequencing or reversal problems, saying *saw* for *was,* or *tip* for *pit.* This is because they have trouble focusing on the order of letters in words.

Sight Words • Learning new words as whole words and remembering them is a special problem for some students. For them, one spelling looks no more right than another. Half of English spellings are irregular, and the uniqueness of each word is confusing to recognize (why can't *cough* be spelled *kof?*).

Oral Reading • Students with learning difficulties often read word-by-word, embarrassed because they know their reading makes little sense. They use context clues to guess at unfamiliar words instead of using word analysis skills, and are anxious about failing and making mistakes. They sometimes use incorrect words with similar sounds or looks, unaware that the meanings are different (*horse* for *house*).

Home Practice • Not doing homework or practicing outside the lessons often compounds reading problems. Having little self confidence, students often hesitate to even try reading or writing without the support of their tutors or teachers.

Writing Difficulties

Many struggling students have problems communicating through writing, so they put off writing tasks whenever possible. Those with weak language skills have no sense of how a story or essay is constructed—a main idea backed up by supporting details, explanations, implications, and so forth.

Handwriting • Many students with learning problems resist writing anything, embarrassed by poor handwriting. Their writing is often sloppy and difficult to read. For many it's a real struggle to write because they have trouble telling their fingers how to formulate the letters. Others can't write well because they can't remember what the letters look like, and to them sizes of letters, spacing, or position on a line are not things that draw attention.

Spelling • Some students often show persistent problems in spelling. Even for those who spell phonetically, the spelling does not look the way it should. Spelling is an enigma, especially with multi-syllabic words.

Capitalization, Punctuation, Grammar • These are problems for those who do not understand sentence or paragraph structure and grammar. Students often use capital and lower case letters inappropriately and know little of what punctuation marks to use.

Comprehension Difficulties

Comprehension is often a problem, and students with learning difficulties make similar comprehension mistakes while listening and while reading. As noted earlier, these students try so hard to decode words that they often have little idea of what they read. Most are slow to comprehend the full meaning of new information. Thus they resist going on to new lessons where they feel less secure. Some are more attuned to the details they read and others to the main idea. Some don't understand because the reading vocabulary is too sophisticated for their limited language skills. Often they guess when questions are asked because they don't understand and are trying to please you.

Problems with Sequencing/Following Directions

Many students can follow through on one-step directions, but have problems with sequencing several directions or items. They have trouble following any list of procedures whether given orally or in writing.

Social Issues

Some students with learning difficulties find social situations—whether in a class or in personal relationships—difficult.

Low Self-esteem • Students often tell of being in special classes as youngsters, bitter about their treatment in school, resentful of being called dumb and stupid, and now they consider themselves dumb and stupid. They fear failing and making mistakes, and feel insecure about making even simple decisions.

Speaking Weaknesses • These students often have limited vocabulary, even mispronouncing words, occasionally using inappropriate humor. They make grammatical errors, and sometimes have difficulty organizing what they want to say (so they don't come to the point) or get stuck on words (as in when you want to introduce your boss to a friend but you can't for the life of you remember her name). There is trouble with word retrieval—their minds seem to go blank as they try to recall words they want to say. And they often have trouble continuing on one topic. They often misjudge whether it is appropriate to say something or interrupt.

Listening Weaknesses • While trying to listen to any conversation, they have difficulty understanding and retaining large amounts of spoken language.

Mathematics Difficulties

Students with learning difficulties may have problems with mathematics, such as not understanding the basic concept of addition or subtraction, not remembering math facts, or not understanding even simple mathematical calculations. Some even count on their fingers (which is fine, but immature), or read numbers backwards because they don't know which digit to concentrate on first, e.g. 17 for 71, 25 for 52. Others learn simple addition but have problems with "carry overs," having trouble remembering in which direction to work. Many have trouble making change and maintaining their checkbooks. Some are confused by math problems, especially if there are several steps in a process and if there is also reading involved.

Life-Related Issues

Some students will bring their personal, family, or work-related problems to you or to the class. Of course you will be empathic and listen, but remember that you are there to help them with their reading/writing problems, not to be their counselor or therapist.

Most adults want learning to be relevant to their everyday lives, giving them skills that will help them in daily tasks, in relationships, at work, and in their communities. It is understandable that our adult students with learning problems want their lessons to be useful immediately.

Job-Related Issues • For many struggling readers, it is hard to find jobs and, once found, to keep them. They're fearful of making mistakes, being scolded, and being "put down" again and again. Getting jobs that match up to their ability and skill levels is frustratingly difficult.

CREATING A LEARNER PROFILE

To help you focus on the specific needs of individual students, it's helpful to create a learner profile, identifying which characteristics described above apply to each student. By analyzing the results of the *READ* test, and observing students' work and actions at your teaching sessions, you can note each student's specific needs in terms of what he or she needs to learn and how he or she learns best. If you note problems with your students' vision and hearing levels, report that to your program director.

With individual learner profiles in hand, you can locate which of the targeted instructions noted on the following pages would be helpful for each student. Keep the learner profiles in the students' portfolios.

LEARNER PROFILE

Learner profiles will help you focus on the specific needs of individual students, identifying which characteristics apply to each student. By observing their work, their actions at your teaching sessions, and noting the results of diagnostic testing, you can see their specific needs. Check characteristics that are appropriate and note the pages for targeted instructions where you will find suggestions for help.

Student's name _____ Date _____

Visual problems ☐ yes ☐ no If yes, describe _____

_____

Hearing problems ☐ yes ☐ no If yes, describe _____

_____

☐ Learning strengths to utilize in instruction . . . . pages 151–157

_____

_____

☐ Diagnostic test to identify strengths and where help is needed . . . . pages 121, 151–152

_____

_____

Problem areas	Targeted instruction
☐ Difficulty focusing	pages 144, 152
☐ Longer time to process information	pages 75–76, 145, 153
☐ Memory difficulties	pages 75–76, 145, 153
Reading difficulties	pages 40–65, 145–146, 153–156
☐ Decoding words (phonics)	pages 51–57, 145, 154–155
☐ Difficulty segmenting individual sounds in words	pages 52–57, 154
☐ Rhyming problems—patterned words	pages 58–64, 155, 179–190
☐ Multi-syllabic word problems	pages 64, 65, 146, 153
☐ Reversals	pages 121, 146, 155
☐ Sight words	pages 46–49, 121, 146, 156
☐ Oral reading (fluency)	pages 77–79, 86, 146, 156
☐ Home practice	pages 125, 146, 156
Writing difficulties	pages 82–90, 111–117, 146, 156
☐ Composition	pages 85, 91
☐ Sentence and paragraph structure	
☐ Vocabulary	page 79, 80

Comments:

_____

_____

_____

_____

TARGETED INSTRUCTION—WAYS TO HELP

All learners have strengths as well as areas where they need help. This section focuses on how to help those who struggle to grasp reading. Learner-centered, individualized, direct instruction is important to helping those with special needs. Regular lesson planning and teaching based on the student's goals are the tutor's responsibility, and it's important for students with learning problems to experience success as soon as possible. The tutor should be in charge especially at the early stages, avoiding independent work for the students until tasks are thoroughly understood. Your job includes finding an appropriate teaching site that is within the comfort zone of the students, has sufficient light, and is free from unnecessary distractions.

Most adults, even those with learning difficulties, are not *total* nonreaders. They've survived, even though they have had to struggle. One of your jobs is to find their strengths and help them take pride in what they *do* know and *what they do well.* Is your student highly motivated? Is he dependable, attending class on time, calling you if there's a problem? Doing homework? What are her reading strengths and learning styles? Does he respond well to phonics instruction? Have a fairly good sight word vocabulary? Good comprehension skills? Ask questions when uncertain?

Seeing these skills listed on the learner profile sheet will be a source of pride and motivation for your students. You also need to find the gaps, the places where your students need help, and to find the best ways to fill these gaps. With a completed learner profile, you can match the needs for each student to the following suggested targeted instructions.

Assessments and Test Taking

This program encourages you to use *READ,* a reading diagnostic test, to help you identify the specific strengths and needs of individual students. Test taking brings anxiety to all of us, but it is terrifying to those with learning difficulties. Explain that there is no "pass-fail," but we are trying to identify what each student already knows and where help is needed. We're looking for outcomes in the post-tests, what each student has learned, but we need a base, a pre-test, to identify what they knew before the teaching began. A diagnostic test tells specifically what skills the students have already mastered and where the gaps are.

Specific tests indicating each student's reading level are required by most states especially where funding is given. Be respectful when giving adult students grade level equivalents, for they may be embarrassed. Explain that these are just a way of measuring or finding out what they know so you know where to start, and that adults have more life experiences than children so they are far more competent and independent.

Having given a diagnostic test, you know the strengths and the needs of your students. You know where the gaps are—which letter-sounds you can focus on, which sight words need reinforcement, whether there are problems with reversals, with rhyming. You will know the approximate reading and comprehension level of each student. Having found these gaps, you can fill them, but build on your students' strengths as well.

When it's time for your students to take a post-test or a test in another situation—perhaps in a class or in a workplace setting—help your students learn how to take tests, especially those with multiple choice questions.

- Complete the easy questions first.
- Skip questions when they're not sure of the answers.
- Go back to the unanswered questions.
- Watch the time, so they can determine where they should spend remaining time.
- Find out if they are penalized for incorrect answers. If they are not penalized, guess. If penalized, leave the answers blank.

Difficulty Focusing

When students have problems focusing on lessons, concentrate only on one specific task—listening—without having them take notes or write at the same time. Keep goals attainable within a relatively short time period, writing them down so that both you and the students can refer to them occasionally. Teach in smaller chunks, giving students opportunities to master these smaller parts before going on to a new task, e.g. teach five new words at one session rather than ten or twenty. Be satisfied with slow, steady progress.

When starting a new task, discuss it first. New readers, especially those with problems, don't like surprises. A new lesson seems like a risk for them. They have little confidence that they can do it.

When giving a new task to students with learning problems, remember these suggestions:

- Model the task for them, talking your way through it.
- Give them confidence by doing it together.
- Give them the opportunity and plenty of time to do it under your supervision. Repetition and practice are so important.
- Use many support materials, e.g., color to highlight a new word stem.
- Encourage them to take responsibility for doing it on their own.

If the pictures on the page are distracting your student from the print, cover the pictures. If there is just too much print on the page and the student is overwhelmed, cover up all but one line at a time.

Remember that movement helps catch attention. Building words with scrabble tiles is a great strategy to keep things moving. Do a word search in the newspaper and see how many times the student can find and circle the word "milk," or any word starting with "m." Use writing as a way of introducing a reading word. Draw a picture to go with the word. Be creative!

Have a quiet place for your lesson—even humming ultraviolet lights can be distracting to some students. Be aware of wearing bright colored clothing or attention getting jewelry, or having a cluttered desk or busy bulletin boards. All of these can distract your students from the task at hand.

Longer Time to Process Information

Go at a slower pace. Struggling students often need as much as three times the time—for reading, for writing, and for processing new information. When you ask a question, know that they usually need extra time to process an answer. Try to use fewer words, in shorter sentences. Pause between thoughts, so that one can be processed before a new thought comes along.

Memory Difficulties

Many students with learning difficulties find that if a tutor or teacher spends a few minutes explaining or paraphrasing new printed material, or if that tutor reads it aloud, the students can get the meaning and more easily remember it. This is especially true if the tutor has primed the student by asking the student to tell all that he or she already knows about the subject to be read. This way the new information gets linked with what the student already knows.

There are many "helps" for memory—recordings, calendars, lists. One can repeat again and again any lesson that has been recorded; appointments can be kept on calendars; lists (even picture lists) help jog the memory for what one planned to do or get. When you give a homework assignment, write it down, and read it aloud together.

It's easier to remember small chunks of information rather than big pieces. Few of us could remember a ten digit number, but we can remember three or four. That's why telephone numbers are "chunked"—384-933-2728. Just so, "chunk" things to be remembered into smaller bits that can be remembered more easily. Five new words or rhyme patterns may be all a student can handle at once before becoming confused. So, be careful not to teach too much too fast. Review often. And hook new ideas, or new words, onto old ones that are already known. Give students plenty of time to process new information.

Finally, don't forget about good old mnemonics and visualization. To remember to buy milk, eggs, and nuts at the grocery store, either try to visualize the three aisles you have to walk down, or create the mnemonic MEN for the three items. It works for most people.

Index cards are wonderful for limiting distractions as students try to memorize. Put one item on each index card, and learning will be much more rapid than learning from a list. Remember not to overwhelm students with too many cards. A few items learned deeply is much better than many learned poorly.

Reading Difficulties

A big percentage of people discover how to read on their own. Since your students have not discovered the principles of reading, you will have to be very direct in your instruction, explaining and modeling every single step.

When teaching basic reading skills, you can blend word decoding with a life style approach. If you give students an opportunity to read what *they* want, they may be able to use their new skills in their daily lives.

Because those with learning difficulties often find it difficult to distinguish individual words, you might put two spaces between words if you're typing or a longer space than normal when printing. Using a ruler or blank paper under each line as it is being read can reduce distraction. For extreme cases, you might even use a paper marker that has a 6 inch cut-out section so that your students focus on only a few words at a time.

You might want to reread Chapter 3, Teaching Reading—Word Identification and Decoding, to remind yourself of techniques that can be helpful.

Decoding Words • Remember the importance of the relationship between letters and sounds, blending them into syllables and words. Take one step at a time. If you have a small group or class, know that it's helpful to take some time to work individually with struggling students.

Focus on small chunks, teaching the sound-symbols that your students missed in the diagnostic test. Be sure students have mastered one step before you take them to the next step in any sequence of learning. Don't be surprised that you must often repeat each step several times.

When two letters, such as *b* and *d* are confused, it is helpful to teach them at different times. Teach one letter for a few lessons to mastery, then introduce the other. When you do bring them back together, you might make all the *b*s yellow and all the *d*s red. Color helps many to distinguish differences.

Another way to help distinguish *b* from *d* is to present them vertically:

b

d

But if the confusing letters are *p* and *b*, the differences are more noticeable if they are placed side by side:

p b

To help students focus on individual letters and sounds, you might highlight all of the same initial letters in one color. Perhaps every *s* could be highlighted in red and every *m* in blue. Ask your students to color every *s* on the page red and every *m* blue and model reading each sound before they read the word. Stretch out the letter sound as you're sounding out a new word to give students more processing time.

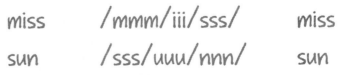

miss   /mmm/iii/sss/   miss

sun   /sss/uuu/nnn/   sun

Some students prefer to listen, spell, and then read.

When teaching word patterns, use colors to help struggling students see the same patterns in words. Highlight the letter stems that are the same.

Use all the support materials available—colored markers to highlight specific letters or words, underlining, audio recorders to help distinguish sounds. For students for whom sounding out a whole word is just too much, read the word to them, cut up the word (the initial letter and the letter stem), and have the student reassemble the letters into a word. By reassembling, the students are focusing on initial letters and on letter stems in pattern.

If your students have problems with multi-syllabic words in the spoken language, break those longer words down into smaller units, individual syllables. Some students find it difficult to do this. Suggest that they tap with a pen on the table or clap their hands to distinguish between syllables as you say the words.

> *e-mer-gen-cy* (four taps or claps)
> *re-frig-er-a-tor* (five taps or claps)

If more help is needed, you might want to explore other reading programs especially designed for structured instruction, such as the Wilson Method, or the Orton-Gillingham Multisensory Method.

Reversals • Some students have reversal problems. When they see the word *top*, they say *pot*, or *ten* instead of *net*. You might want to focus on the word by pointing to or by coloring the first letter to be read, asking for that sound. It is helpful to some students to actually put a finger on that first letter to keep them focused on it. This usually provides the needed clue. If they can't give the sound, ask for the name of the letter. You might also remind them to think of what word makes sense in the context of the story.

Sight Words • Using 3x5 cards for individual word study is always good, but some students who have trouble remembering words find that they remember them better if they associate them with pictures. On individual 3x5 cards, either paste a picture or draw a simple stick figure on one side and write the word carefully in manuscript on the other side.

Many students find they remember lists of words taught by sight better if they are grouped into categories that cue recognition, such as colors, sizes, animals, or pieces of clothing.

You may want to use some or all of the techniques described in the Visual-Auditory-Kinesthetic-Tactile (VAKT) approach. This approach has been around for years and has been helpful in many cases. (See Appendix, page 199.)

Oral Reading • Many students with reading problems have trouble reading aloud and may be reluctant to try. They may read better silently. De-emphasize oral reading. It often interferes with comprehension while embarrassing poor readers. At the same time, oral reading is essential, first for the teacher to hear where students need help, and second for students to gain confidence in reading aloud as a life skill. Do give your students an opportunity to practice reading a selection silently before you ask them to read it aloud. Give them time to self-correct. If a student hesitates on a word for more than one second, give him or her the word so that reading can continue as fluently as possible. If your students read word-by-word, you may want to try putting slash marks around phrases. Encourage them to read the phrases silently before reading them aloud. Rereading a passage three times boosts fluency and self-confidence enormously.

If you are working in a small group or a class, be sensitive to students' feelings of embarrassment, and let them volunteer to read aloud. You might suggest that the group read aloud together at first, then as dual readings before individual readings, always using interesting materials that are well within their reading abilities. You might want to show pauses with slash marks, or suggest that your students read or sing along with a recording.

Home Practice • Many students haven't done homework since childhood. They may find it difficult to take time from their often busy home and work schedules to settle down to study. Write down short but explicit assignments. You might suggest that they work for only ten to fifteen minutes each day, noting it on their calendars to remind them. Giving assignments pertinent to their daily lives and interests, such as reading a simple sports story or an article on comparative costs of food, shows them the practicality of their work.

Explaining and agreeing on a Student/Tutor Agreement (see Appendix, page 196) often motivates students to do home practice. Some have such little self-confidence that they hesitate to try to work independently, even for ten minutes, without the tutor's supervision. Give very short assignments at first, and give well deserved praise when they complete any home assignments. Make sure the homework is easy enough to complete independently.

Writing Difficulties

Adults who find writing difficult should not be expected to do too much writing at one time. It is so hard for them to direct their hands that they can't concentrate on the ideas they want to express. Rereading Chapter 5—Writing might help refresh your memory of techniques already described.

Mapping (see page 85) is an effective way to help learners who have trouble organizing written stories or reports. Ideas are written down, circled, and linked to the main subject by a line. New ideas are added. Then the students can put those ideas in sequence, actually making an outline to guide them in their writing.

Because adults want their learning to be relevant to their daily lives, find real purposes for writing—shopping lists, journal writing, letters, directions to a special place. Concentrate first on content. Capitalization and punctuation can wait until later.

Handwriting • Adult students who are new writers often leave little or no space between words, making it difficult to read individual words. Suggest that a bigger than normal space be left between words, perhaps having them put a finger down after each word to make sure there's enough space Have your students write only on every other line. If a student has problems holding a thin pen or pencil, look for one that is thicker, get a pencil gripper, or wrap rubber bands around the pen about an inch from the point.

Spelling • Students with spelling problems are encouraged by success when they work with words in pattern. Knowing that *m-an* spells *man,* gives them the pattern for spelling many words when they know consonant sounds; not only simply spelled words like *pan, tan, ran,* but the beginning of multi-syllabic words like *manage* or *manufacture.*

Students are frightened of words with several syllables. Break those multi-syllabic words into individual syllables, saying each syllable separately. Students often find they can give a good try to spelling these smaller segments. They may have trouble spelling *satisfying,* but breaking it down and saying "Spell *sat-is-fy-ing,*" often helps them have the confidence to try longer words. Try actually using scissors to cut long words into syllables, move them around, and have your students put them back in the correct order.

Keeping a checklist of misspelled words helps to identify error patterns. Is the problem putting the right sounds in the right order? If so, ask students to visualize the word on a theatre marquee, trace it in the air or you trace it on their backs. Try drawing a dash for each sound they hear in the word, then adding the letters. Is the problem remembering what words look like? If so, encourage invented spellings which you can correct later. For those who need more reinforcement, you could suggest that your students actually trace the word as written by you several times, saying the word as they write. Putting Scotch tape over your model makes the image fade, and students commit the word to memory as they "trace."

Capitalization, Punctuation, Grammar • Eventually your students must learn where to capitalize letters, what punctuation to use, and more about grammar. There are suggestions in Chapter 5, but don't get bogged down in spelling, punctuation, capitalization, and other form errors until your students have the confidence to put down their thoughts in writing.

Computers • Our students are often concerned about errors, left-out or inappropriate words, and spelling. Using computers as word processors gives them the freedom to make errors, since errors are easily corrected. They can then redirect their efforts toward expression.

Using computers is a self esteem booster as well as a good way to supplement and practice basic skills, especially phonetic and word recognition skills. Keyboard writing often allows students to express their thoughts more easily than writing by hand (often they can't read their own handwriting), for they don't have to be concerned with forming letters correctly or with messy writing.

Check with your local library to see if they have supplemental software that supports basic literacy skills. Your students may be able to go there to reinforce the skills you're teaching. If your students' learning difficulties include vision problems, you might want to search out computer programs that scan the printed page and deliver a talking voice. The text on a computer may be made easier to read by changing the font, the size, and even the color. Also, there are speech to text (your student speaks, the computer types) and other talking software and devices available, including talking dictionaries that define words as the student reads. You'll find specific software suggestions on page 205 in the Appendix.

These technologies can help students learn basic skills. They also give students access to information they need when they are not advanced enough to read it themselves.

Comprehension Difficulties

While you are focusing on smaller chucks of reading, don't overlook that most important component of reading, comprehension. Introduce reading comprehension material using controlled vocabulary as soon as possible. Make sure to preview reading material by first asking the student to share what he or she already knows on a topic. Bringing out what they know helps students associate the new information with what is already understood. This improves comprehension and memory. Don't forget to underline, circle, or color code important information to make it stick out and become more memorable.

Ask open-ended questions—who, what, where, when, why, how—rather than questions that can be answered by "*yes*" or "*no*" (closed questions). Pre-reading questions let struggling students know what to look for as they read. If they can't answer questions about an entire article accurately, ask questions on smaller and smaller chunks—paragraphs or even sentences. Be sure to explore the main concepts just as much or more than details. It is the main gist that remains in our memories, while details quickly fade away.

Encourage your students to think about whether what they read makes sense. After you've read something to your students, or after they've read it, ask them to paraphrase or put it in their own words, even at the basic sentence level. They may have to hear or read that same information several times—be patient.

Problems with Sequencing/Following Directions

To help your students understand sequencing, you might ask them to tell you in detail, step by step, how they'd do something (wash dishes or a car, find a specific program on TV, brush their teeth). This is really "task analysis" and can prepare them for further sequential tasks.

Several steps given at one time often confuse students with learning difficulties. Take one step at a time, and present information in a natural sequential manner.

Explain each step, showing how each step builds on the next step. When you're giving directions, start with something that has only two steps (Pick up the book, open it to page 53). Move on to more complicated things, such as giving driving instructions—"Go straight for two blocks, turn left on Main Street, go two blocks to the stop sign, turn right, the restaurant is on the right," five steps.

There are many simple sequential things that students can read, such as directions on a cake mix box or directions for putting a tool or toy together. Have your students give you simple directions to a gas station or to the library. Most people's limit is five to nine instructions at a time.

In Chapter 5 there are other suggestions, such as writing a sequential sentence or a short story with several logical steps. *(John was reading a book. The phone rang. He jumped to answer the phone. The cat ran too. John tripped over the cat. He missed the phone call.)* Cut the story up, each sentence on a separate slip of paper, and have the students put them in logical order. You can also cut comics up and have your students put them in the proper sequence.

When you're giving an assignment or homework to a student, you might write out your own "task analysis" of that task, that is, the specific steps that must be done in sequential order. We sometimes assume our students can do a specific assignment. More often they need the help of step-by-step instructions.

Social Issues

While our focus is on the reading and writing problems of those with learning difficulties, tutors and teachers must be aware of the social issues some of our students face.

Low Self-Esteem • The Language Experience Approach (see page 41) is a positive way to introduce persons with learning difficulties to a comfortable learning situation. It is non-threatening because it focuses not on the problems but on the goals, the dreams, the strengths of the individual. Giving adults who have struggled all their lives with reading an opportunity to share *their* thoughts, putting those thoughts on paper, can be a first step toward self confidence and self esteem.

Be careful not to embarrass your students or suggest laziness when their pace is not as fast as others. Reduce the emphasis on competition or perfection.

As your students see their reading and writing skills improve, they will overcome their fear of making mistakes, and decision making will become easier. They need lots of support and praise for even small successes.

Speaking Weaknesses • Vocabulary grows when individuals interact with others, when they read more. When students mispronounce words or speak with grammatical errors, focusing on those mistakes usually makes them withdraw, unwilling to expose themselves by speaking. Simply modeling the correct grammatical structures gives students opportunities to *hear* standard English—eventually most will follow your lead. However, if students ask you to correct their speech, respect their requests.

If they have difficulty organizing what they want to say, you might suggest that your students jot down notes or draw simple pictures to remind themselves and help them keep their thoughts together. This will also help them stay focused on one topic and organize their thinking. If they have trouble retrieving words or thoughts, just wait. Be patient.

Listening Weaknesses • Most of us have trouble processing and remembering details in long lectures. Students with learning difficulties have problems processing new information in what we might consider shorter lectures or instructions. Break your instructions down into smaller parts, even modeling the task, or use pictures as reminders. Ask your students to paraphrase or put in their own words what you've said. You'll notice that their listening comprehension gradually gets stronger as you work together.

Support

Adults who have had few successes in life need praise and assurance that they're actually doing something worthwhile and correct. Give honest praise for even small parts of work done. Reward effort and progress even though the results were not perfect. There are so many ways to give praise and support— saying *Good! – Well done! – Right on! – Great! – You did it right the very first time! – Aren't you proud of that?*—or you could give a "high five" if it's appropriate, or even a big smile of encouragement. Praise students' specific target skills and accomplishments at the end of each session, so they go home with a positive attitude and clear pride in the specific success that they experienced. Respect the uniqueness of each student and value different learning styles.

Teach (give support), reteach (give praise), evaluate (share the good points with the students), review (continue with encouraging words). Don't take a new step until the previous one was learned, and let your students know of progress no matter how little.

Mathematics Difficulties

While mathematical problems are real to students with learning difficulties, and you as tutors and teachers must be aware of this, math deficiencies are not addressed in this book. Many books include lessons to help those with math problems. Search in book stores, or ask your librarian for help in finding appropriate books. Be sensitive to the fact that you are working with adult students, and be sure that the books are not childish but appropriate for real life situations.

You might want to suggest that your students get calculators and use real money and the calculators in real-life shopping situations. The most important part of mathematics remediation is to help students understand the concepts (for example, of a 15–20% tip), rather than the calculations. Calculators can always be used in practical situations, but your students still need to be able to reason about whether one item or another is the best buy, or whether a purchase will deplete the checking account.

Life-Related Issues

If students bring personal, family, or work-related problems to class, listen respectfully and suggest that they talk to your program coordinator who can direct them to where they can get appropriate help. Refocus them on the tasks at hand.

They may want help writing a letter to a collection agency or reading a letter from the tax authorities. This may be well beyond their present skills, but acknowledge their request for help. You might make these requests a focus of a lesson, demonstrating that their newly-learned reading and writing skills can be helpful in their daily lives.

Job-Related Issues • Many employers are willing to hire non- or poor readers, especially if they know that the prospective employees are working to improve their education. However, reading grade level means nothing to employers. Instead, they'd like to know what these non- or poor readers can do. In the Appendix (see page 204) is a list of *Workplace Skill Requirements Met by New Readers*. It lists jobs that can be done by adults with specific grade level reading skills. Remember also that some employers are happy to give oral rather than written directions to an employee with specific talents needed on the job. An annual review can be read to the employee. The employee could dictate to someone else what to write (for example, when explaining to a new TV owner how to use the remote). Accommodations can be requested, if they don't cause any major disruption to the operation of the workplace.

Employers are seeking employees with specific talents who will be loyal, punctual, and good citizens on the job. If our students have used computers, even in simple ways, that may open access to jobs that involve computer use. Other talents, such as carpentry, car mechanics, or plumbing also open doors. Make sure to help your students build on these other talents—it will help them land the jobs they want. This is why using real life materials—job applications, reading instruction manuals—adds to the skills and self-confidence of poor readers as they apply for and/or hope to upgrade their jobs.

Getting jobs that match your students' abilities and skill levels can be frustrating. But letting your students know that there are jobs out there, jobs for which they can qualify, is often the motivation they need to keep working.

Appropriate Materials

As you look for materials for students with learning problems to read, keep these things in mind:

- Make sure the material looks like adult material. Kid stuff is a put down.
- Bigger print and simple fonts are easier to read, so look at font style and size.
- It's easier to focus when there is more white space. Avoid solid print.
- Pictures give ideas of what the print is about.
- Look at the length of the books or articles. Shorter is better.

- Subject matter pertaining to real life—sports, health issues, household interests, workplace information—is most meaningful to adults.
- Look for books that build sequentially one skill on another.
- Instructions should be chunked into manageable parts.
- If using a "how to" manual, check to be sure that the instructions are detailed and simply written.
- If your students are parents of small children, they might be interested in books they can read to their children. Select books that are not only age appropriate for the children but also at a reading level that is comfortable for your students.

You might want to use the five finger test to figure out whether a text is at the appropriate level. As a student reads 100 words, have the student put up one finger for every word that he or she can't read. When five fingers are in the air, the text is too difficult and frustrating to continue with. Find a book with lower level vocabulary. Remember that lower level vocabulary does *not* mean lower level thoughts. You can find excellent history, science, science fiction, sports, "how to," and other books written for adults but with elementary reading vocabulary. These are called "high interest/low vocabulary" books.

You might want to experiment with books on tape/CDs, because many students seem to get more meaning from listening to text, or listening while following the print, than from only reading it.

SUMMARY

One of the most important things you can do to help those with learning problems is to slow down your teaching. Give new information in smaller doses, breaking big tasks into little ones. Plan your lessons well, but be willing to change them when necessary. Don't hesitate to try out new techniques. Review, review, review.

When students don't seem to "get it" with a specific teaching technique, we tend to repeat and repeat. Yes, repeat several times, but you might want to attack the problem in a different way. Remember, one method does not fit all.

Involve your students in intervention. They often have wonderful insights into how they learn best. Ask them and try to incorporate their favorite methods into your teaching, honoring what they know about how they prefer to go about learning.

Often students with learning problems become dependent on instructors. This can make them feel even more helpless. Our goal is to make the students independent. There is a fine line between being there for help and support and making them dependent on us. Homework geared toward practicing what a student knows should help build independence.

And finally, look at the Table of Contents of this book. You probably will find suggestions that you had overlooked in your first reading.

TUTOR READINESS EVALUATION

Are You Ready to Tutor?
Attitudes
Tutoring Strategies
Assessment and Evaluation
Lesson Planning
Case Histories

Summary

BEFORE YOU BEGIN TO INSTRUCT A STUDENT, you should be able to evaluate your attitudes as well as your knowledge of the information and skills you will need to provide successful instruction in basic reading and writing.

This chapter is a self-check evaluation to help you assure yourself that you either know information or instruction skills directly or that you know where to locate that information in this book.

ARE YOU READY TO TUTOR?

Attitudes (See Chapter 2.)

1. Are you free of critical attitudes toward teenagers and adults who cannot read or have limited reading and writing skills? Do you really understand the problems? With absolute honesty, examine your own attitudes toward those who have reading/writing limitations.

2. Are you willing to be patient with small gains? Can you accept the need for a long period of instruction before functional literacy is attained?

3. Can you be enthusiastic enough in your instruction to provide genuine encouragement, so your students can have a sense of accomplishment with the many small successes they must attain before any long-term success can be achieved?

4. Do you recognize that you as a tutor are a learner in many situations?

5. Do you honestly understand and believe the philosophy that meaning is the base of literacy instruction?

6. Do you understand the changing roles of tutors and students in collaborative instruction? Are you willing to work at developing these role changes in yourself and in your students?

Tutoring Strategies

1. Can you describe the basic steps in Language Experience? (See Chapter 3.)

2. Why is it important to start with oral language? (See Chapter 1.)

3. How would you help a student create a personal word list? (See Chapter 3.)

4. What steps would you use to teach the letter sound relationships your students need to know? (See Chapter 3.)

5. What are some examples of words appropriate to teach in pattern and how would you teach them? (See Chapter 3.)

6. What are the six steps in the writing process? (See Chapter 5.)

7. Do you know how to teach comprehension from the very first lesson? (See Chapters 1 and 4.)

8. How would you identify your students' long-term and short-term goals? (See Chapter 6.)

Assessment and Evaluation (See Chapter 8.)

1. When will you assess your students?
2. How will you assess your students?
3. What types of things do you need to be assessing?
4. Can you describe the contents and purposes of a student's portfolio?
5. Can you explain the relationship between assessment and instruction?

Lesson Planning (See Chapter 8.)

Below are the descriptions of several students typical of those who receive instruction in basic literacy. Read each case carefully noting the information given. Then jot down what you think you would do if such a student were assigned to you. Answer the following questions:

1. What supplies and books would you have with you?
2. How would you find your student's strengths and needs?
3. How would you identify your student's goals and interests?
4. What strategies would you use to teach?
5. From what you know about this individual, suggest a focus for beginning instruction.
6. Identify suitable written material for the student to read.
7. How would you include writing in your lessons?
8. How else could you help this student?
9. What further assessment tools would you use?

Case Histories

Student 1: Mr. B. • Mr. B. is 21 years old, married, with one child. He works at a foundry and says he had four years of schooling. He is eager but shy and gentle; very polite and cooperative.

The initial interview and your personal assessment showed that Mr. B. could not read one word and that he did not know the names or sounds of any letters. His reading proficiency range is beginning. He is interested in gardening.

If Mr. B. were assigned to you, what steps would you take to plan the instructional strategy?

Student 2: Mr. P. • Mr. P. is 55 years old, single. He is an unemployed migrant worker and is in Grade 1 class in Adult Basic Education (ABE). He will continue at ABE, but he needs individual help.

He has had no previous schooling. He wants to get a job, get a driver's license, and read his school work. He is most cooperative and intelligent; however, he lacks confidence.

The initial interview and your personal assessment showed that he reads only print from his environment, such as the names of fast food places and only the common road signs such as *STOP* and numbers pertaining to speed and highway numbers. His reading proficiency range is beginning.

If Mr. P. were assigned to you, what steps would you take to plan the instructional strategy?

Student 3: Ms. V. • Ms. V., 32, is a single mother of three small children. She works at a local garment plant as a seamstress. She went to school for ten years in a small town. Ms. V. was offered a better job but could not accept it because her reading and writing skills were at such a low level. Even first level supervisory jobs at her plant require the ability to write evaluations.

Ms. V. is eager and enthusiastic. She seems intelligent, is self-confident and cooperative. She desperately wants to learn and needs help. The initial interview and your personal assessment showed that she reads well at the intermediate range, but her writing is unintelligible. She is very intimidated by writing. Your personal interview showed that she wants to read to her children.

If Ms. V. were assigned to you, what steps would you take to plan the instructional strategy?

Student 4: Mr. J. • Mr. J. was assigned to you but very limited information was given. In fact, all you know is his name and telephone number. Arrangements were made for your first meeting.

What will you do to prepare for this first meeting? How best can you use this hour? Jot down the questions you plan to ask and the information you plan to share about yourself.

Create your own student and describe your plan for instruction for the next meeting.

Student 5: Mrs. E. • Mrs. E. is a 62-year-old widow whose husband had always taken responsibility for household and business affairs. She suddenly finds herself in a position where she has to balance her checkbook, pay bills, and write letters such as canceling credit cards, transferring Social Security benefits, etc. She likes to read simple inspirational stories from religious magazines. Even though she can read well at an advanced proficiency range, she finds herself overwhelmed at what she is facing at this traumatic time in her life.

If Mrs. E. were assigned to you, what steps would you take to plan the instructional strategy?

SUMMARY

There's no "fail or pass" in this check-list evaluation. You have evaluated your own attitudes, your own tutoring strategies, your own ability to assess and evaluate students who might be assigned to you. You've made lesson plans for typical students. You surely now feel confident and ready for actually meeting your first students. New friendships will be formed, and you'll find you'll be learning as well as teaching.

EPILOGUE: ON DOWN THE ROAD

One-to-One
Small Groups
Classroom Settings
Making a Difference

THE GOAL OF THIS BOOK is to offer you, the tutor, a basis from which to become an effective instructor. I hope it has helped you gain many useful skills. These skills should enable you to be successful with your very first student. However, it is only as you use your skills again and again that you will become really proficient as a reading and writing tutor/teacher. As you work, you will create, adapt, and find new ways to help your students. Do take advantage of continued in-service training. Whether you teach one-to-one, in a small group, or in a classroom setting, let's look at what you can expect within a short time of tutoring/teaching.

ONE-TO-ONE

After a few months together in one-to-one sessions, most tutors and students have become friends. They've found things of mutual interest and concern, and they feel free to discuss personal and even controversial subjects. Even their greetings are personal: "How is Bobby feeling?" Or a student can't wait to tell his tutor good news: "You'll never guess—I got a promotion at work!" or "I got a reply from that letter I wrote asking for information on bus travel."

There are many advantages to one-to-one tutoring, just as there are advantages to teaching in small groups or in classroom settings. Many new tutors are hesitant to try teaching more than one student, and many students are more comfortable when they have their own private teacher. They feel the pace can be adjusted to their own needs and abilities. Another big advantage to both tutor and student in one-to-one tutoring is simpler scheduling. It is easier for two people to adjust or postpone meetings when other responsibilities or sickness come up. In addition, tutors may want to continue the lessons by letter, encouraging students to respond to letters with written assignments that can be corrected by a return letter from the tutor. E-mail can also be an effective way to communicate.

Finally, although the tutor has a lesson plan, students know that they can ask for immediate help in whatever area they indicate. One day they may want to work on a job application, another on a note to a child's teacher, and yet another on reading and discussing an article about the local baseball team.

SMALL GROUPS

In small group sessions, students can learn from each other as well as from the tutor. Less pressure is put on an individual to perform or respond to every question. New relationships are formed, and students build self confidence. They learn that others have reading and writing problems similar to their own.

If you were to walk into a collaborative small group session after the group had been working together for a few weeks, you might be greeted by the following scene. Two learners are discussing their papers with each other, reading parts aloud, asking questions, listening, and providing feedback. In another part of the room, a learner is listening to a recording and writing at the same time. The tutor and a fourth learner are spending some time working with capitalization. After a few minutes, the tutor joins the person with the recording and then is called to join the two learners discussing their papers.

Doesn't look like group work, does it? But you have walked in on this group at a time during their two-hour session when learners have been through a group sequence and are now doing things they can do alone, with a tutor, or with a peer. Other parts of the lesson will involve the whole group.

CLASSROOM SETTINGS

Classrooms just mean more students. There is still the same dynamic between people who want help in reading and writing and someone who has been trained and is willing to teach.

The Language Experience Approach can easily be adapted to a classroom situation by putting the choice of a topic to a vote, with the learners interacting to agree on a story. Techniques of teaching basic reading and writing are the same and can easily be adapted to a classroom situation. Let the students decide by voting which key words they want for letter-sound practice. There'll be plenty of discussion and interaction, just what you want. A class can be divided into smaller special study groups where the more advanced students can help those who struggle. Peer teaching can be another form of learning.

MAKING A DIFFERENCE

> I am only one,
> But still I am one.
> I cannot do everything,
> But still I can do something;
> And because I cannot do everything
> I will not refuse to do the something that I can do.
> *Edward Everett Hale*

Whether you teach one-to-one, in a small group, or in a classroom setting, your life will change, and you will have touched the life of at least one other person. But in reality you may have influenced many lives—students' children, families, friends, co-workers. Who knows how far the ripple effects may go?

As you are out there, sometimes feeling alone and insignificant, as you contemplate the overwhelming task of teaching millions to read and write, remember that there are thousands of tutors/teachers sitting as you are, teaching one-to-one, teaching in small groups, teaching in classrooms. You are indeed opening new doors; you are breaking down barriers—cultural, economic, educational, and racial. Good luck, and know that together we will make a difference.

APPENDIX

A

D'Nealian™ Alphabet

Learner Goals and Interests

Learner's Stated Goals

Reading/Writing Inventory

Lesson Plan

Continuous Lesson Plan

Suggested Key Words—Phonics

Word Patterns

Three Hundred Most Frequently Used Words, in Rank Order

Signs in Capital Letters

Useful Words for Filling Out Forms

Personal Word List

Student/Tutor Agreement

Listening Skills

Critical Thinking Strategies

Visual-Auditory-Kinesthetic-Tactile (Vakt) Approach

Tuckman's Model of Group Process

Checklist for Evaluation of Adult Basic Reading Material

Workplace Skill Requirements Met by New Readers

Technology and Computer Resources for Adult Literacy

D'NEALIAN™ ALPHABET

D'NEALIAN™ MANUSCRIPT ALPHABET

a b c d e f g h i j k l m

n o p q r s t u v w x y z

A B C D E F G H I J K L M

N O P Q R S T U V W X Y Z

D'NEALIAN™ CURSIVE ALPHABET

a b c d e f g h i j k l m

n o p q r s t u v w x y z

A B C D E F G H I

J K L M N O P 2

R S T U V W X Y Z

D'NEALIAN™ NUMBERS

0 1 2 3 4 5 6 7 8 9

From *D'Nealian Handwriting* by Donald N. Thurber. Copyright © 1981 by Scott, Foreman and Company. Reprinted by permission.

LEARNER GOALS AND INTERESTS

TO THE TUTOR/INTERVIEWER: You need to know why learners are in the program, and what their expectations and interests are as you work together to plan lessons.

Directions: During an informal discussion, ask learners why they are in the program and what they might like to do once they can read and write better. Do not read this list to learners. Record each learner's stated goals or check off topics as mentioned. After the session transfer the information to the intake form. This Goals and Interests summary becomes part of the learner's portfolio.

LEARNER'S STATED GOALS

_____

_____

_____

_____

_____

_____

COMMUNITY (1)

☐ Apply for citizenship
☐ Read/write for newsletter
☐ Read for community activities
☐ Participate in neighborhood watch
☐ Read for religious activities (Bible, Talmud, etc.)

VOTING (2)

☐ Register to vote
☐ Read ballot and vote

DRIVER'S LICENSE (3)

☐ Apply for driver's license
☐ Receive license
☐ Take driver's test

GED (4)

☐ Register for GED classes
☐ Complete GED

JOB/BETTER JOB (5)

☐ Read classified ads
☐ Apply for armed services
☐ Read notes from co-workers
☐ Read work-related materials
☐ Read manuals
☐ Read equipment operating instructions
☐ Fill out applications
☐ Take test for a job
☐ Write notes to co-workers
☐ Write reports
☐ Fill out orders/requisitions

SURVIVAL SKILLS (6)

- ☐ Read menus
- ☐ Read recipes
- ☐ Write shopping lists
- ☐ Read/write letters
- ☐ Read cooking directions/food labels
- ☐ Read newspapers/magazines
- ☐ Read bills
- ☐ Write checks
- ☐ Balance checkbook against statement
- ☐ Open/use checking/savings accounts
- ☐ Apply for safe deposit box
- ☐ Apply for unemployment insurance
- ☐ Complete credit/loan application
- ☐ Read lease/rental agreement

- ☐ Read medication labels/prescriptions
- ☐ Read labels in drug store
- ☐ Apply for Medicare/Medicaid/HMO
- ☐ Fill out insurance forms
- ☐ Read bus/airline/train schedules
- ☐ Read travel guides/maps
- ☐ Read car repair invoices
- ☐ Read info in phone book & Yellow Pages/find number, address
- ☐ Read novels, magazines
- ☐ Read in a special interest area:
  - ☐ Sports
  - ☐ Gardening
  - ☐ Fashion
  - ☐ Health
  - ☐ Finance
  - ☐ Sewing, knitting
- ☐ Other

PARENTING SKILLS (7)

- ☐ Read notes from school
- ☐ Read to child
- ☐ Read/write cards/letters
- ☐ Participate in scouting program

- ☐ Write notes to school
- ☐ Help child with homework
- ☐ Participate in PTA/PTO

OTHER EDUCATION/TRAINING (8)

- ☐ Enter training program
- ☐ Take Adult Basic Education (ABE) classes

- ☐ Enter Adult Basic Education (ABE) program
- ☐ Apply for college

LIBRARY/CREATIVE (9)

- ☐ Apply for library card
- ☐ Check out books
- ☐ Use reference materials

- ☐ Read in library
- ☐ Check out A/V materials
- ☐ Write journal, stories, poems, essays

Date _____

Learner's name _____

Interviewer _____

READING/WRITING INVENTORY

AS THE TUTOR/INTERVIEWER, you might say: "This list of questions is about what you do read or write or what you might like to read or write. We'll be talking about newspapers, books, magazines, and other materials like letters, advertisements, school notices, and signs."

Date _____

Learner's name _____

Interviewer _____

A. General: "Do you usually read any of the following?" If "yes," ask, "How often?" (*Read this list to learner.*)

KIND	DAILY	WEEKLY	SEVERAL TIMES A MONTH
Business letters			
Personal letters			
School notices			
Ads			
Grocery lists			
Menus			
Television guides			
Job directions			
Application forms			
Books to children			
Junk mail			
Other			

B. *Newspapers*: "Have you looked at any newspapers in the last six months?" If "no," go to C. If "yes," ask, "What part of the paper? How often do you read it?" (*Do **not** read this list to the learner.*)

KIND	DAILY	WEEKLY	SEVERAL TIMES A MONTH
Front page			
Local news			
Sports page			
Ads			
Comics			
Obits			
Lifestyle			
Advice columns			
Horoscopes			
Letters to the editor			
Other			

C. *Books*: "Have you looked through any books in the last six months?" If "no," go to D. If "yes," ask, "What kinds of books? How often do you read them?" (*Do **not** read this list to the learner.*)

KIND	DAILY	WEEKLY	SEVERAL TIMES A MONTH
Manuals			
Mysteries			
Romances			
Sports			
Cookbooks			
Gardening			
Religious			
Other			

D. Magazines: "Have you looked at any magazines in the last six months?" If "no," go to E. If "yes," ask, "What kinds of magazines? How often do you read them?" (*Do **not** read this list to the learner.*)

KIND	DAILY	WEEKLY	SEVERAL TIMES A MONTH
How to			
Romances			
Sports			
Gardening			
Women's			
Fashion			
Hunting/fishing			
News			
Other			

E. Reading Materials for Lessons: "Of the kinds of reading materials that we just talked about, are there any you would like to use in our lessons? Which ones?" (*Circle the ones the learner mentions.*)

F. Writing: "Do you usually write any of the following?" If "yes," ask, "How often?" (*Read this list to the learner.*)

KIND	DAILY	WEEKLY	SEVERAL TIMES A MONTH
Grocery lists			
Business letters			
Notes at work			
Personal notes			
Notes to school			
Letters/cards			
Journal/diary			
Catalog orders			
Work reports			
Checks			
E-mails			
Other			

LESSON PLAN

Student's name: _____   Lesson #: _____   Lesson date: _____

Tutor's name: _____   Length of lesson: _____

Lesson goal/objectives _____

_____

_____

Review homework _____

_____

	This session	*Next session*
Review previous lesson		
New work or work in progress		
Activities		
Homework		
Reading for pleasure		
Student comments		
Tutor notes		

CONTINUOUS LESSON PLAN

SOME TUTORS HAVE LIMITED TIME for lesson planning. After they have formed an initial lesson plan, they can "continuous plan" by using a loose leaf or spiral notebook, putting the initial information on the left side of the first page, and moving on to the next column for the next lesson. You can quickly see what is needed for the next lesson and continue planning page after page.

Student's name _____ Tutor's name _____

Date of first lesson _____

Goals/objectives _____

	SESSION DATE/HOURS	SESSION DATE/HOURS	SESSION DATE/HOURS
Review homework			
Review previous lesson			
New work or work in progress			
Activities			
Homework			
Reading for pleasure			
Student's comments			
Tutor notes			

SUGGESTED KEY WORDS—PHONICS

For use when teaching initial consonant sounds

As you use phonics, keep these three items in mind:

- Teach only the letter-sound relationships each individual student needs—those identified in the student's assessment.

- Suggest as possible key words those the students can best relate to. Ask the students to pick the key word.

- Remember that English is not a phonetically regular language. Some consonants have more than one sound or may behave irregularly. For example, the letter *c* has the /k/ sound (e.g. *corn, camera*) but it also has the /s/ sound (e.g. *ceiling, city*). Also, the letter *k* has no sound (e.g. *knife, know*, etc.).

B	bus, baby, ball, bed, banana, bag, bird
C	cat, cup, can, cake, comb, coffee / cigar, city, cent, celery
D	dog, dish, doll, desk, doughnut
F	fish, fan, fire, feet, feather
G	gas, girl, game, gate, garage / gem, gentleman, giraffe
H	hand, hat, house, ham, horn, hi-fi
J	jar, jacket, jet, jug, jeep
K	key, kite, king, kerchief
L	leg, lamp, lock, leaf, ladder, leather
M	man, motor, money, milk, mother
N	name, nose, nail, needle
P	pot, pan, pig, pants, pipe, pumpkin, pen
Q(QU)	quarter, queen, quilt, quick
R	rat, radio, rocket, rope, river, red
S	sun, sink, socks, sandwich
T	telephone, towel, table, tub, turkey, tea
V	valentine, valley, violin, vacuum, van
W	window, wing, wig, watch, wagon, water
X*	wax, fix, box, tux
Y	yellow, yarn, yo-yo, yardstick
Z	zipper, zebra, zoo

Digraphs

CH	church, chair, children / cholesterol, chemical, choir
CH	chute, chauffeur
PH	phone, photo, pharmacy
SH	shoe, ship, shower, shovel
TH	this, the, them, these / thumb, thank, theater
WH	wheel, whale, white

*There are no words in English that begin with *x* as it makes the /ks/ sound.

WORD PATTERNS

SHORT A SOUNDS

-ab	-ack	-ad	-ag	-am	-amp	-an	-and	-ang	-ank
cab	back	ad	bag	am	camp	an	and	bang	bank
dab	hack	bad	gag	ham	damp	ban	band	fang	rank
gab	jack	cad	hag	jam	lamp	can	hand	gang	sank
jab	pack	dad	lag	clam	champ	fan	land	hang	tank
lab	rack	fad	nag	slam	clamp	man	sand	rang	yank
nab	sack	had	rag	swam	cramp	pan	gland	sang	blank
tab	tack	lad	sag		stamp	ran	grand	tang	clank
blab	black	mad	tag		tramp	tan	stand	clang	plank
flab	slack	pad	wag			van		slang	crank
slab	crack	sad	brag			clan			drank
crab	track	clad	drag			plan			frank
drab	shack	glad	flag			scan			spank
grab	whack	shad	shag			span			thank
scab	smack		snag			than			
stab	snack		stag						
	stack								

-ap	-ash	-asp	-ass	-ast	-at	-atch	-ath	-ax
cap	ash	asp	ass	cast	at	catch	bath	ax
gap	bash	gasp	bass	fast	bat	hatch	path	wax
lap	cash	hasp	lass	last	cat	latch	wrath	flax
map	dash	rasp	mass	mast	fat	match		
nap	gash	clasp	pass	past	hat	patch		
rap	hash		brass	vast	mat	thatch		
sap	lash		grass	blast	pat			
tap	mash		class		rat			
chap	rash		glass		sat			
clap	sash				vat			
flap	clash				brat			
slap	crash				chat			
snap	smash				flat			
trap	stash				slat			
	trash				scat			
					that			

SHORT E SOUNDS

-eck	-ed	-eg	-elf	-ell	-elp	-elt	-em	-en	-end
deck	bed	beg	elf	bell	help	belt	hem	den	end
Heck	fed	egg	self	dell	yelp	felt	them	hen	bend
neck	led	keg	shelf	fell		melt	stem	men	lend
peck	red	leg		hell				pen	mend
check	wed	peg		sell				ten	send
speck	bled			tell				glen	blend
	fled			well				then	spend
	sled			yell				when	trend
	shed			quell					
	sped			shell					
				smell					
				spell					
				swell					

-ent	-ept	-ess	-est	-et
bent	kept	less	best	bet
dent	wept	mess	nest	get
lent		bless	pest	jet
rent		chess	rest	let
sent		dress	test	met
tent			vest	net
went			west	pet
spent			chest	set
			crest	wet
			quest	yet
				fret

SHORT I SOUNDS

-ib	-ick	-id	-ift	-ig	-ilk	-ill	-im	-in	-inch	-ing
bib	kick	bid	gift	big	bilk	bill	dim	in	inch	bing
fib	lick	did	lift	dig	milk	fill	him	bin	cinch	ring
rib	nick	hid	rift	fig	silk	gill	rim	din	pinch	sing
crib	pick	kid	sift	jig		hill	skim	fin	clinch	wing
	sick	lid	drift	pig		kill	slim	kin		bring
	tick	rid	shift	rig		mill	swim	pin		fling
	wick	grid	swift	wig		pill	trim	sin		sling
	brick	skid		brig		rill	whim	tin		sting
	trick	slid		swig		sill		win		swing
	chick					till		chin		thing
	thick					will		shin		
	click					chill		thin		
	flick					drill		grin		
	slick					grill		skin		
	quick					quill		spin		
	stick					spill		twin		
						skill				
						still				

-ink	-int	-ip	-ish	-iss	-ist	-it	-itch	-ive	- ix
ink	hint	dip	dish	hiss	fist	it	itch	give	fix
pink	mint	hip	fish	kiss	list	bit	ditch	live	mix
sink	tint	lip	wish	miss	mist	fit	pitch		six
wink	flint	nip	swish	bliss	twist	hit	witch		
blink		rip				kit	stitch		
slink		sip				lit	switch		
stink		tip				pit			
think		zip				sit			
		yip				wit			
		chip				grit			
		ship				mitt			
		whip				quit			
		flip				skit			
		slit				spit			
		slip				twit			
		grip							
		trip							
		quip							
		skip							
		snip							

SHORT O SOUNDS

-ob	-ock	-od	-og	-oll	-on	-ond	-ong	-ot	-ox
cob	cock	cod	bog	doll	on	bond	bong	cot	ox
fob	dock	god	cog	loll	don	fond	gong	dot	box
gob	hock	hod	dog	moll	non	pond	long	got	fox
job	lock	nod	fog		yon		song	hot	
rob	mock	pod	hog				tong	not	
mob	pock	rod	jog				wrong	pot	
sob	rock	sod	log				strong	rot	
blob	sock	clod	clog					blot	
slob	tock	plod	frog					clot	
snob	clock	shod	smog					plot	
	flock							slot	
	crock							shot	
	frock							spot	
	shock							trot	
	smock								
	stock								

SHORT U SOUNDS

-ub	-uck	-ud	-uff	-ug	-ull	-um	-ump	-un	-unch
cub	buck	bud	buff	bug	cull	bum	bump	bun	bunch
dub	duck	cud	cuff	dug	dull	gum	dump	fun	lunch
hub	luck	mud	huff	hug	gull	hum	hump	gun	punch
nub	muck	stud	muff	jug	hull	mum	jump	nun	brunch
pub	puck	thud	puff	lug	lull	rum	lump	pun	crunch
rub	suck		bluff	mug	mull	sum	pump	run	
sub	tuck		gruff	pug	null	glum	clump	sun	
tub	chuck		stuff	rug	skull	slum	plump	shun	
club	shuck			tug		drum	slump	spun	
grub	cluck			chug		scum	stump	stun	
stub	pluck			thug		chum	thump		
	stuck			plug					
				slug					
				smug					

-ung	-unk	-up	-us	-ush	-usk	-ust	-ut	-uzz
dung	bunk	up	us	gush	dusk	bust	but	buzz
hung	dunk	cup	bus	hush	husk	dust	cut	fuzz
lung	hunk	pup	plus	lush	tusk	just	gut	
rung	junk	sup	thus	mush		lust	hut	
sung	sunk			rush		must	jut	
clung	chunk			blush		rust	nut	
flung	drunk			flush		crust	rut	
stung	flunk			plush			shut	
swung	skunk			slush			brush	
							crush	
							shush	

LONG A SOUNDS

-ace	-ade	-age	-aid	-ail	-aim	-ain	-aint	-ait	-ale
ace	fade	age	aid	ail	aim	gain	faint	bait	ale
face	jade	cage	laid	bail	maim	main	paint	gait	dale
lace	lade	page	maid	fail		pain	saint	wait	gale
mace	made	rage	paid	hail		rain	quaint	trait	hale
pace	wade	sage	raid	jail		vain			kale
race	blade	wage	braid	mail		brain			male
brace	glade	stage		nail		drain			pale
place	grade			pail		grain			sale
space	shade			rail		train			tale
	spade			sail		chain			vale
	trade			tail		plain			scale
				vail		slain			shale
				wail		stain			stale
				frail					whale
				quail					
				snail					
				trail					

-ame	-ane	-ape	-ase	-aste	-ate	-ave	-ay	-aze	-eigh
came	cane	ape	base	baste	ate	cave	bay	daze	eight
dame	lane	cape	case	haste	date	gave	day	faze	sleigh
fame	mane	gape	vase	paste	fate	nave	gay	gaze	weigh
game	pane	nape		taste	gate	pave	hay	haze	
lame	sane	rape		waste	hate	rave	jay	maze	
name	vane	tape		chaste	late	save	lay	raze	
same	wane	drape			mate	wave	may	blaze	
tame	crane	grape			rate	brave	nay	glaze	
blame		shape			sate	crave	pay	graze	
flame					crate	grave	ray		
frame					grate	shave	say		
shame					plate	slave	way		
					skate		clay		
					slate		play		
					state		fray		
							gray		
							tray		
							stay		
							sway		

LONG E SOUNDS

-e	-ea	-each	-ead	-eak	-eal	-eam	-ean	-eap	-east	-eat	-eech
be	pea	each	bead	beak	deal	beam	bean	heap	east	eat	beech
he	sea	beach	lead	leak	heal	ream	dean	leap	beast	beat	leech
me	tea	peach	read	peak	meal	seam	lean	reap	feast	feat	
we	flea	reach	plead	weak	peal	team	mean	cheap	least	heat	
she	plea	teach		bleak	real	cream	wean			meat	
		bleach		freak	seal	dream	clean			neat	
				speak	veal	gleam	glean			peat	
					zeal					seat	
					steal					cheat	
										cleat	
										pleat	
										treat	
										wheat	

-eed	-ee	-eef	-eek	-eel	-eem	-een	-eep	-eet	-ief	-y
deed	bee	beef	leek	eel	deem	keen	beep	beet	brief	carry
feed	fee	reef	meek	feel	seem	seen	deep	feet	chief	marry
heed	see		peek	heel	teem	teen	jeep	meet	grief	bunny
need	tee		reek	keel		green	keep	fleet	thief	funny
seed	wee		seek	peel		queen	peep	greet		sunny
weed	free		week	reel		sheen	seep	sheet		
bleed	tree		cheek				weep	sleet		
breed	glee		creek				creep	sweet		
creed	thee		sleek				sheep	tweet		
freed	three						sleep			
greed							steep			
speed							sweep			
steed										
tweed										

LONG I SOUNDS

-ice	-ide	-ie	-ife	-igh	-ight	-ike	-ild	-ile	-ime
lice	bide	die	life	high	fight	bike	mild	file	dime
mice	hide	lie	rife	nigh	light	dike	wild	mile	lime
nice	ride	pie	wife	sigh	might	hike	child	pile	time
rice	side	tie		thigh	night	like		rile	chime
vice	tide	vie			right	mike		tile	crime
slice	wide				sight	pike		vile	grime
spice	bride				tight	spike		smile	slime
twice	glide				bright			while	
	slide				fright				
					flight				
					plight				
					slight				

-ind	-ine	-ipe	-ire	-ise	-ite	-ive	-y	-ye
bind	dine	pipe	ire	rise	bite	dive	by	dye
find	fine	ripe	dire	wise	kite	five	my	eye
hind	line	wipe	fire		mite	hive	cry	lye
kind	mine	gripe	hire		site	live	dry	rye
mind	nine	swipe	mire		quite	chive	fly	
rind	pine		sire		spite	drive	ply	
wind	tine		tire		white		fry	
blind	vine		wire				shy	
grind	shine						sky	
	spine						sly	
	swine						spy	
	thine						sty	
	twine						thy	
	whine						try	

LONG O SOUND

-o	-oach	-oad	-oal	-oam	-oan	-oast	-oat	-obe	-ode	-oe	-oke
go	coach	goad	coal	foam	loan	boast	oat	lobe	ode	doe	coke
no	poach	load	goal	loam	moan	coast	boat	robe	bode	foe	joke
so	roach	road		roam	roan	roast	coat	globe	code	hoe	poke
		toad			groan	toast	goat		mode	toe	woke
							moat		rode	woe	yoke
							bloat				bloke
							float				choke
							gloat				smoke
											spoke

-old	-ole	-olt	-ome	-one	-ope	-ose	-ost	-ote	-ove	-ow
old	dole	bolt	dome	bone	cope	hose	host	note	cove	bow
bold	hole	colt	home	cone	dope	nose	most	rote	dove	low
cold	mole	dolt	Nome	lone	hope	pose	post	tote	rove	mow
gold	pole	jolt		pone	mope	rose		vote	wove	row
hold	role	volt		tone	rope	chose		quote		sow
mold	stole			zone	scope	those				tow
sold				shone	slope	close				blow
told				stone						flow
										glow
										slow
										crow
										grow
										show
										snow

LONG U SOUND

-ew	-ule	-use	-ute
few	mule	use	cute
hew	yule	fuse	mute
blew		muse	flute
flew			
slew			
chew			
crew			
drew			
grew			
stew			

OTHER SOUNDS IN WORD PATTERNS

-all	-alk	-ar	-arch	-arge	-ark	-arm	-arn	-arp	-arsh
all	talk	bar	march	barge	bark	farm	barn	carp	harsh
ball	walk	car	parch	large	dark	harm	darn	harp	marsh
call	chalk	far	starch	charge	hark	charm	yarn	sharp	
fall	stalk	jar			lark				
gall		par			mark				
hall		tar			park				
mall		scar			shark				
tall		star			spark				
wall					stark				
small									
stall									

-aught	-aul	-aunch	-aunt	-ause	-aw	-awl
caught	haul	haunch	gaunt	cause	caw	awl
naught	maul	launch	haunt	pause	jaw	bawl
taught		paunch	jaunt	clause	law	brawl
		staunch	taunt		maw	crawl
			vaunt		raw	shawl
					saw	
					chaw	
					claw	
					flaw	
					draw	

-en	-er	-ern
brighten	either	fern
dampen	fatter	stern
darken	matter	
freshen	poorer	
hasten	richer	
lengthen	scatter	
shorten		
silken		

-ew	-ird	-irl	-irt	-oard	-oice	-oil	-oin	-oint	-oise
dew	bird	girl	dirt	board	voice	oil	coin	joint	noise
Jew	gird	swirl	shirt	hoard	choice	boil	loin	point	poise
new	third	twirl	skirt			coil			
brew		whirl	squirt			foil			
crew						soil			
drew						toil			
grew						broil			
chew						spoil			
flew									
slew									
stew									

-oist	-oo	-ood	-ook	-ool	-oom	-oon	-oop	-oost	-oot
foist	boo	food	book	cool	boom	boon	coop	boost	boot
hoist	coo	mood	cook	fool	doom	coon	hoop	roost	hoot
joist	moo	brood	hook	pool	loom	goon	loop		loot
moist	too		look	drool	room	loon	droop		root
	zoo		nook	spool	zoom	moon	troop		toot
	shoo		took	stool	gloom	noon	scoop		scoot
			brook		groom	soon	stoop		shoot
			crook			spoon	swoop		
			shook			swoon			

-ooth	-or	-ord	-ore	-ork	-orm	-orn	-ort	-orth	-ouch
booth	or	cord	ore	cork	form	born	fort	forth	ouch
tooth	for	ford	wore	fork	norm	corn	sort	north	couch
	nor	lord	chore	pork	storm	horn	tort		pouch
			score	York		morn			vouch
			swore	stork		torn			
						worn			

-ought	-ould	-ound	-our	-ouse	-out	-outh	-ow	-owl
ought	could	bound	four	house	out	mouth	bow	owl
bought	would	found	pour	louse	bout	south	cow	cowl
fought	should	hound		mouse	gout		how	fowl
sought		mound			pout		now	howl
brought		pound			shout		vow	jowl
thought		round			spout		wow	yowl
		sound			stout		plow	
		wound			trout			
		ground						

-own	-sion	-tion	-ude	-ue	-uke	-ull	-une
down	collision	action	dude	rue	duke	bull	dune
gown	decision	attention	nude	sue	Luke	full	June
town	division	fraction	rude	blue		pull	tune
brown	occasion	mention	crude	clue			
crown	television	motion		glue			
clown		nation		true			
frown							

-ush	-ute
bush	lute
push	flute

THREE HUNDRED MOST FREQUENTLY USED WORDS, IN RANK ORDER

the	has	also	day	high	going	need
of	when	did	same	upon	look	four
and	who	many	another	school	asked	within
to	will	before	know	every	later	felt
a	more	must	while	don't	knew	along
in	no	through	last	does	point	children
that	if	back	might	got	next	saw
is	out	years	us	united	program	best
was	so	where	great	left	city	church
he	said	much	old	number	business	ever
for	what	your	year	course	give	least
it	up	way	off	war	group	power
with	its	well	come	until	toward	development
as	about	down	since	always	young	light
his	into	should	against	away	days	thing
on	than	because	go	something	let	seemed
be	them	each	came	fact	room	family
at	can	just	right	though	president	interest
by	only	those	used	water	side	want
I	other	people	take	less	social	members
this	new	Mr.	three	public	given	mind
had	some	how	states	put	present	country
not	could	too	himself	think	several	area
are	time	little	few	almost	order	others
but	these	state	house	hand	national	done
from	two	good	use	enough	possible	turned
or	may	very	during	far	rather	although
have	then	make	without	took	second	open
an	do	world	again	head	face	God
they	first	still	place	yet	per	service
which	any	own	American	government	among	certain
one	my	see	around	system	form	kind
you	now	men	however	better	important	problem
were	such	work	home	set	often	began
her	like	long	small	told	things	different
all	our	get	found	nothing	looked	door
she	over	here	Mrs.	night	early	thus
there	man	between	thought	end	white	help
would	me	both	went	why	case	sense
their	even	life	say	called	John	means
we	most	being	part	didn't	become	whole
him	made	under	once	eyes	large	matter
been	after	never	general	find	big	

Henry Kucera and W. Nelson Francis, *Computational Analysis of Present-Day American English* (Providence: Brown University Press, 1967).

SIGNS IN CAPITAL LETTERS

A minimum list of words and phrases one should be able to read for physical safety, social acceptability, and avoidance of embarrassment.

GENERAL SIGNS

ADULTS ONLY

ANTIDOTE

BEWARE

BEWARE OF THE DOG

BUS STATION

BUS STOP

CAUTION

CLOSED

COMBUSTIBLE

CONTAMINATED

CONDEMNED

DANGER

DEEP WATER

DENTIST

DON'T WALK

DO NOT CROSS, USE TUNNEL

DO NOT CROWD

DO NOT ENTER

DO NOT INHALE FUMES

DO NOT PUSH

DO NOT REFREEZE

DO NOT SHOVE

DO NOT STAND UP

DO NOT USE NEAR HEAT

DO NOT USE NEAR OPEN FLAME

DOCTOR (DR.)

DOWN

DYNAMITE

ELEVATOR

EMERGENCY EXIT

EMPLOYEES ONLY

ENTRANCE

EXIT

EXPLOSIVES

EXTERNAL USE ONLY

FALLOUT SHELTER

FIRE ESCAPE

FIRE EXTINGUISHER

FIRST AID

FLAMMABLE

FOUND

FRAGILE

GASOLINE

GATE

GENTLEMEN

HANDLE WITH CARE

HANDS OFF

HELP

HIGH VOLTAGE

IN

INFLAMMABLE

INFORMATION

INSTRUCTIONS

KEEP AWAY

KEEP CLOSED AT ALL TIMES

KEEP OFF (THE GRASS)

KEEP OUT

LADIES

LOST

LIVE WIRES

MEN

NEXT (WINDOW GATE)

NO ADMITTANCE

NO CHECKS CASHED

NO CREDIT

NO DIVING

NO DOGS ALLOWED

NO DUMPING

NO FIRES

NO LOITERING

NO FISHING

NO HUNTING

NO MINORS

NO SMOKING

NO SPITTING

NO SWIMMING

NO TOUCHING

NO TRESPASSING

NOT FOR INTERNAL USE

NOXIOUS

NURSE

OFFICE

OPEN

OUT

OUT OF ORDER

PEDESTRIANS

PROHIBITED

POISON

POISONOUS

POLICE (STATION)

POST NO BILLS

POST OFFICE

POSTED

PRIVATE

PRIVATE PROPERTY

PULL

PUSH

SAFETY FIRST

SHALLOW WATER

SHELTER

SMOKING PROHIBITED

STEP DOWN (UP)

TAXI STAND

TERMS CASH

THIN ICE

THIS END UP

THIS SIDE UP

UP

USE IN OPEN AIR

USE OTHER DOOR

USE BEFORE (DATE)

VIOLATORS WILL BE PROSECUTED

WALK

WANTED

WARNING

WATCH YOUR STEP

WET PAINT

WOMEN

Reprinted with permission of Corlett T. Wilson and the International Reading Association.

TRANSPORTATION SIGNS

ALL CARS (TRUCKS) STOP

ASK ATTENDANT FOR KEY

BEWARE OF CROSS WINDS

BRIDGE OUT

BUS ONLY

CAUTION

CONSTRUCTION ZONE

CURVE

DANGEROUS CURVE

DEAD END

DEER (CATTLE) CROSSING

DETOUR

DIM LIGHTS

DIP

DO NOT BLOCK WALK (DRIVEWAY)

DO NOT ENTER

DRIFTING SAND

DRIVE SLOW

EMERGENCY VEHICLES ONLY

END 45

END CONSTRUCTION

ENTRANCE

EXIT ONLY

EXIT SPEED 30

FALLING ROCKS

FLOODED

FLOODS WHEN RAINING

FOUR WAY STOP

FREEWAY

GARAGE

GATE

GO SLOW

HOSPITAL ZONE

INSPECTION STATION

JUNCTION 101A

KEEP TO THE LEFT (RIGHT)

LANE ENDS

LAST CHANCE FOR GAS

LEFT LANE MUST TURN LEFT

LEFT TURN ON THIS SIGNAL ONLY

LEFT TURN ONLY

LEFT TURN O.K.

LOADING ZONE

LOOK

LOOK OUT FOR CARS (TRUCKS)

LISTEN

M.P.H.

MECHANIC ON DUTY

MEN WORKING

MERGE LEFT (RIGHT)

MERGING TRAFFIC

MILITARY RESERVATION

NEXT

NO PARKING

NO LEFT TURN

NO PASSING

NO RIGHT TURN

NO RIGHT TURN ON RED LIGHT

NO SMOKING AREA

NO STANDING

NO STOPPING

NO TURNS

NO "U" TURN

NOT A THROUGH STREET

ONE WAY DO NOT ENTER

ONE WAY STREET

PAVEMENT ENDS

PLAYGROUND

PROCEED AT YOUR OWN RISK

PRIVATE ROAD

PUT ON CHAINS

R.R.

RAILROAD CROSSING

REST ROOMS

RESUME SPEED

RIGHT LANE MUST TURN RIGHT

RIGHT TURN ONLY

ROAD CLOSED

ROAD ENDS

SCHOOL STOP

SCHOOL ZONE

SLIDE AREA

SLIPPERY WHEN WET (FROSTY)

SLOW DOWN

SLOWER TRAFFIC KEEP RIGHT

SPEED CHECKED BY RADAR

STEEP GRADE

STOP

STOP FOR PEDESTRIANS

STOP WHEN OCCUPIED

STOP MOTOR

THIS LANE MAY TURN LEFT

THIS ROAD PATROLLED BY AIRCRAFT

THREE WAY LIGHT

TURN OFF

TURN OFF 1/2 MILE (1/4 MILE)

TRAFFIC CIRCLE

TRUCK ROUTE

UNLOADING ZONE

USE LOW GEAR

WATCH FOR FLAGMAN

WATCH FOR LOW FLYING AIRCRAFT

WINDING ROAD

YIELD

YIELD RIGHT OF WAY

USEFUL WORDS FOR FILLING OUT FORMS

Date	Zip Code	Divorced	Weekly
Month	City	Widowed	Part-time
Year	State	Single	Full-time
Name	Telephone number	Occupation	Temporary work
Mr.	Business telephone	Employer	Sex
Mrs.	Home telephone	Firm	Male
Miss	Citizen	Place of employment	Female
Ms.	Citizenship status	Self-employed	Health plan coverage
First name	Birth date	Length of service	Medical history
Last name	Date of birth	References	Physical impairment
Maiden name	Place of birth	In case of emergency	Driver's license number
Middle name	Age	Education	Signature
Middle initial	Height	Years of schooling	Residence
Address	Weight	Last school attended	Insurance
Street	Social Security number	Degrees held	Dependents
Permanent address	Marital status	Diplomas held	E-mail
Mailing address	Married	Salary	Present address
	Separated	Hourly	

PERSONAL WORD LIST

Name _____

STUDENT/TUTOR AGREEMENT

For a period of _____ weeks, from _____ to _____

Tutor agrees to:

_____

_____

_____

_____

_____

_____

_____

_____

Student agrees to:

_____

_____

_____

_____

_____

_____

_____

_____

_____

Dated _____   Tutor _____

Student _____

LISTENING SKILLS

AT THE BEGINNING of each lesson, take time to talk with your students to find out their feelings and opinions about the lessons and what is happening in their lives. This time is well spent and will reap the benefits of increased learning.

Effective listening will be the basis of communication with your students. You can practice listening skills in your lessons by keeping the focus on your students and their concerns. Here are some important listening skills that you should know and use.

A. REFLECTIVE LISTENING • Responding to a person by giving back both the message and the feelings in a tentative manner.

- **Parroting:** Repeating exactly, word for word, what the other person has said.

- **Paraphrasing:** Giving back the speaker's idea in your own words, rather than repeating the speaker's words.

- **Focus Questioning:** Helping the speaker keep to the point he/she is making, asking questions like: "Just what is it that you don't understand?" "What did you like about today's lesson?"

B. ENCOURAGING SKILLS • Letting the speaker know he/she is being heard.

- **Interested Silence:** Helping the speaker talk about a difficult problem, because you give him/her space to think before you react.

- **Door Openers:** Issuing an invitation to the other to speak through cues—silence, or words that indicate you are willing and have the time to listen. Use phrases such as: "You seem troubled." "You sure look excited." "How did it go?"

- **Open-Ended Questions:** Encouraging the speaker to elaborate by bringing ideas to mind that the person isn't aware of. For example, ask "What do you want to do now?" rather than suggesting a course of action.

C. SUMMARIZING • Stating the main points of the other's conversation in two or three sentences.

CRITICAL THINKING STRATEGIES

Teachers can make critical thinking and critical analysis a regular part of all classroom work in the following ways:

- Start with information sources (e.g. articles, advertisements, speeches, dialogues, pictures, videos) that are obviously biased or ideologically loaded, such as an advertising campaign against smoking, and then progress to more subtle examples, such as a play or sitcom that demonstrates negative aspects of smoking.

- Raise awareness by pointing out critical literacy skills when they are exhibited by the teacher or by learners.

- Choose readings or listening, speaking, or writing activities that are relevant and interesting for learners.

- Prompt learners to examine how their own experiences and values relate to and influence their approaches to topics.

- Understand that some learners may feel uncomfortable expressing opinions, especially if this kind of learning approach is new to them.

- Be aware that multiple interpretations of information and different points of view may or may not be represented in classroom texts, materials, and discussions, so choose activities in which learners must consider a variety of perspectives.

- Build in time for learners to become comfortable with texts or activities before asking them to look at them critically.

- Have learners formulate questions as well as answer them.

- Balance instruction in basic literacy skills (e.g. decoding, vocabulary building, predicting, summarizing) with practice in critical analysis skills.

- Provide support for challenging aspects of a task (e.g. pre-practice new vocabulary or grammar points, clarify the main idea of a text, choose a familiar topic, etc.) so that learners can focus on critical or analytical points.

- Use authentic texts (e.g. newspaper articles, advertisements, letters, news broadcasts) and less traditional literacy texts (e.g. graffiti, cartoons, commercials, television sitcoms) whenever possible.

- Shift from an emphasis on finding a right answer to eliciting ranges of interpretations that are supported by sound reasoning and thoughtful examinations.

("Critical Literacy for Adult English Language Learners"—by Carol Van Duzer and MaryAnn Cunningham Florez, National Center for ESL Literacy Education, December 1999)

"This document was produced at the Center for Applied Linguistics (4646 40th Street, NW, Washington, DC 20016 (202-362-0700) with funding from the U.S. Department of Education (ED), Office of Vocational and Adult Education (OVAE), under Contract No. ED-99-CO-0008. The opinions expressed in this report do not necessarily reflect the positions or policies of ED. This document is in the public domain and may be reproduced without permission.)

VISUAL-AUDITORY-KINESTHETIC-TACTILE (VAKT) APPROACH

If learning is difficult for your students, you may want to use some or all of the techniques described in the Visual-Auditory-Kinesthetic-Tactile (VAKT) approach, describing several ways to teach a word. This approach has been around for years and has been helpful in many cases.

Visual • Take a word card and hold it in front of your students saying, "Look at the word, picturing it exactly the way you'd take a picture of a friend. Say the word." (Students respond.) "Now close your eyes and picture the word in your mind. Can you see the word?" (Students respond.) "Now, open your eyes and look at the card again. What is the word?" (Students respond.)

Auditory • Say the word slowly as it appears on the word card. Say it in a phrase or sentence to the learners. Ask them to repeat what you have said. Sometimes the sound of the learners' own voices helps memorization. It may take many repetitions before the learners recognize the word. The goal is to recognize the word, not to pronounce each letter in turn.

Kinesthetic • For words of two, three, or four letters, it is often helpful, if the letters are known, to ask students to use their index fingers to write the word in the air, on the table, or on paper. The letters of that word are thus fixed in the students' minds, and another sensory pathway for recall of the word is provided. Or, ask students to trace over the letters of the word with their fingers. When they have traced the letters several times, remove the copy and have them write the word from memory, saying each part of the word as it is written.

You can use crayons instead of highlighters if your student responds to a kinesthetic or feeling approach, for crayons do give a texture which can be felt.

Tactile • Some students can be helped by forming letters in a pan of sugar or damp sand using the index finger. The feel of rough sand and the pressure needed to form the letters help some students remember the letter forms and the words. You might also use sandpaper or different types of textured materials to help your students feel a letter. This is often an effective way to help a person sense the difference between *b* and *d*.

TUCKMAN'S MODEL OF GROUP PROCESS

STAGES	CHARACTERISTICS	TUTOR'S ROLE	ISSUES
FORMING	Getting acquainted Tentative behavior "What's in it for me?" Testing "Will I fit in?"	**Leader** "Carries the ball" Clearly defines objectives and expectations Accepting of "teacher" focus Supporting interpersonal relationships	Dependence Fear of unknown Trust Looking for authority figure Need for security
STORMING	Conflict Frustration Expressions of emotion Growing independence of individual group members Volatility Increase in student-to-student interactions	**Conflict Manager** Acceptance of the importance of conflict Support Encouragement Attention to student's concerns	Challenge to leadership Need to belong Need for social interaction Need to assert individuality
NORMING	Cooperation Team spirit Expressions of opinions Group unity Shared responsibility Group decision making	**Guider** Promoting democratic procedures Enabling people to take on leadership	Group cohesion
PERFORMING	Productivity Problem-solving Interdependence Maturity	**Resource** Minimum supervision Occasional reinforcement for outstanding achievement Facilitation	Participatory democracy Team work Getting the job done
ADJOURNING	Re-emergence of earlier issue Sadness Celebratory	**Facilitator** Celebrator Sometimes a guider Acceptance of feelings	Resistance to ending Grieving Affirming the group's achievements Closure

CHECKLIST FOR EVALUATION OF ADULT BASIC READING MATERIAL

WHEN FUNDS ARE LIMITED, buying wisely for the affiliate library is a must. Whenever possible, books should be reviewed with certain criteria in mind. To aid you in selecting the most useful publications, we are reprinting (with minor adaptations) the checklist developed by the Basic Education and Reading Committee of the International Reading Association (Anabel Newman and George Eyster, primary researchers; Sam Duazat, chair, 1977; Joye Jenkins Coy, chair, 1978-79).

INSTRUCTIONS

Review the adult reading material carefully. Consider all of the following in your review: the cost, preface, table of contents, introductory instructions to the teacher and/or to the students, print, graphics, index, and all related or supporting materials.

YES NO APPEAL

Is the material:

- ☐ ☐ a. Fresh?
- ☐ ☐ b. Enjoyable to read?
- ☐ ☐ c. Of interest to adults?

RELEVANCE

Does the material:

- ☐ ☐ a. Pertain to adult life experience?
- ☐ ☐ b. Add to the general knowledge of adults?
- ☐ ☐ c. Present, where factual, up to date information?
- ☐ ☐ d. Present language naturally?

PURPOSE

Does the content:

- ☐ ☐ a. Include statements of broad goals and specific objectives?
- ☐ ☐ b. Fit the purpose of the learner?
- ☐ ☐ c. Fulfill a functional purpose?

PROCESS

Does the process deal with:

- ☐ ☐ a. Pre-reading experiences?
- ☐ ☐ b. Word analysis?
- ☐ ☐ c. Well constructed reading passages?
- ☐ ☐ d. A clear progression of ideas or story line?
- ☐ ☐ e. Comprehension?
- ☐ ☐ f. Appropriate vocabulary?
- ☐ ☐ g. Silent reading?
- ☐ ☐ h. Oral reading?

YES   NO   HUMAN RELATIONS
Does the material:

☐ ☐   a. Depict a cultural, ethnic, racial, or gender group in a positive way, avoiding stereotypes?

☐ ☐   b. Represent various current occupations?

☐ ☐   c. Avoid sexist language (e.g., all male or all female nouns and pronouns) when content refers to both sexes?

☐ ☐   d. Present workers in non-stereotypical roles?

☐ ☐   e. Include characters without sexist bias?

☐ ☐   f. Stimulate interpersonal exchanges and evoke discussions?

EVALUATION
Does the material:

☐ ☐   a. Offer suggestions for continuing evaluation of the student's progress?

☐ ☐   b. Provide for pre-tests and post-tests?

FUNCTIONS OF THE MATERIAL
Does the material:

☐ ☐   a. Encourage wide reading?

☐ ☐   b. Suggest other resources and activities for student exploration?

☐ ☐   c. Promote inductive thinking?

☐ ☐   d. Provide student instructions that are clear and understandable?

☐ ☐   e. Give a sense of continuous success and mastery?

☐ ☐   f. Provide an answer key for the teacher?

☐ ☐   g. Provide an answer for the student?

FORMAT
Is the material format:

☐ ☐   a. Usable?

☐ ☐   b. Pleasing and attractive?

☐ ☐   c. Appealing to adult students?

☐ ☐   d. Pictorial or illustrated where appropriate (photographs, drawings, graphs, maps, etc.)?

☐ ☐   e. Presented with ample space between lines and in margins for easy reading?

☐ ☐   f. Set in type (large or medium) appropriate for the material and the student?

YES NO TEACHER DIRECTIONS

Are instructions:

☐ ☐ a. Included for the instructor where needed?

☐ ☐ b. Presented in a self-contained manual where needed?

☐ ☐ c. For the instructor clear where needed?

☐ ☐ d. Included and designed so that teachers do not need special training?

CONTENT

Judgments based upon stated or apparent readability level or design (e.g. 0-3, 3–8, 8–12 grades).

☐ ☐ a. Do the materials provide for appropriate reading level experiences?

☐ ☐ b. Are the selections short enough to hold interest and long enough to give meaning?

☐ ☐ c. Is there recognition of the amount of reinforcement needed at the content reading level?

☐ ☐ d. Does the readability develop at an appropriate rate and by increments?

☐ ☐ e. Are comprehension exercises included?

☐ ☐ f. Are problem-solving selections included?

☐ ☐ g. Are writing activities included and linked to reading selections?

FUNCTIONING LEVEL TABLE*

Educational Functioning Level Descriptors—Adult Basic Education Levels

Literacy Level	Basic Reading and Writing	Numeracy Skills	Functional and Workplace Skills
Beginning ABE Literacy Grade level 0–1.9	No or minimal reading/writing skills. At upper end of range, can recognize and read letters/numbers, some words. Can write limited number of sight words, familiar words, simple messages. Narrative writing frequent errors.	Little or no recognition of numbers/counting skills.	Little/no ability to read basic signs/maps, can provide limited personal information on simple forms. Can handle routine entry level jobs that require little or no basic written communication or computational skills and no knowledge of computers.
Beginning Basic Education Grade level 2–3.9	Can read simple material on familiar subjects; can write simple messages but writing lacks clarity and focus. Some control of basic grammar.	Can count, add, and subtract three-digit numbers; simple multiplication through 12; simple fractions.	Able to read simple directions, signs, maps, fill out simple forms, write phone messages. Minimal computer. Can recognize short explicit pictorial texts, can read want ads, complete simple job applications.
Low Intermediate Basic Education Grade level 4–5.9	Can read text on familiar subjects with simple, clear structure, get meaning from context, follow directions, write simple paragraphs; can self and peer edit for spelling/punctuation.	Can perform with high accuracy four basic math operations (whole numbers up to three digits), can use all basic mathematical symbols.	Can handle basic reading, writing, computational tasks related to life roles such as completing forms, reading simple charts, labels, etc. Can use simple computer programs, follow sequential routine tasks.
High Intermediate Basic Education Grade level 6–8.9	Can read simple descriptions and narratives on familiar subjects, write simple narrative descriptions on familiar subjects, and use basic punctuation. Makes grammatical errors with complex structures.	Can perform all four basic math operations with whole numbers and fractions. Can determine correct math operations for solving narrative math problems.	Can handle all basic life skills, can read authentic materials (simple employee handbooks, payroll stubs), complete job applications, reconcile bank statements, follow simple written instructions and diagrams. Can use most basic computer software.

* **Adapted from the National Reporting Requirements for Adult Education's NRS Implementation Guidelines, 2007**
"The descriptors are entry-level descriptors and are illustrative of what a typical student functioning at that level should be able to do. They are not a full description of skills for the level."

TECHNOLOGY AND COMPUTER RESOURCES FOR ADULT LITERACY

There are educational software programs for beginning as well as for advanced readers. Some programs are more appropriate for basic literacy/adult basic education and others are designed for English for Speakers of Other Languages (ESOL) students. There are programs that help with special needs. Here are some suggested resources for locating appropriate computer or Web-based resources.

General:

- The National Institute for Literacy's LINCs site (Literacy Information and Communication System): *www.nifl.gov/lincs*
- NIFL Technology Special Collection: *www.altn.org/techtraining*
- David Rosen's: The Literacy List and Adult Literacy Education Software Recommendations: *www.newsomeassociates.com*
- Thinkfinity – The Verizon Corporation's education site developed in partnership with ProLiteracy and the National Center for Family Literacy: *www.thinkfinity.org*
- New Readers Press – ProLiteracy: *www.newreaderspress.org*
  - News For You Online: *www.newsforyouonline.com*
  - GED Practice 1120 (CD-Rom)
- HEC Reading Horizons: *www.readinghorizons.com*
- Adult Learning Activities, California Distance Learning Project: *www.cdlponline.org*

ESOL:

- English for All: *www.myefa.org*
- Computers in Action: *tech.worlded.org/docs/cia*

Math:

- The Problem Solver (math newsletter published by SABES – System for Adult Basic Education Support): *www.sabes.org/resources/publications/problemsolver*
- Student/Learner – Numeracy, LINCs Special Collection: *www.literacynet.org/sciencelincs/studentlearner-num.html*

Learning Disabilities:

- Learning Toolbox: Resources to enable students with learning difficulties to become better learners: *coe.jmu.edu/learningtoolbox/*
- Learning Disabilities Association of America: *www.Ldanatl.org*
- Teaching LD Web site: *www.teachingld.org*
- National Research Center on Learning Disabilities: *www.nrcld.org*
- National Center for Learning Disabilities: *www.ncld.org*
- Arizona Department of Education Exceptional Student Services Parent Information Network—Assistive Technology: *www.ade.state.az.us/ess/SpecialProjects/pinspals/documents/AssistiveTech*
- Benetech Bookshare.Org: *www.bookshare.org/web/Welcome.html*

BIBLIOGRAPHY

Abercrombie, M.L.J. (1964). *Anatomy of judgment: An investigation into the processes of perception and reading.* New York: Basic Books.

Applebee, A.N. (1981). *Writing in the secondary school: English and the content areas.* Urbana: National Council of Teachers of English (NCTE).

Applebee, A. & Langer, J. (1983). Instructional scaffolding: Reading and writing as natural language activities. *Language Arts, 60,* 168-75.

Army Management Staff College, Fort Belvoir, VA (199x). Developing thinking skills: Critical thinking. http://www.amsc.belvoir.army.mil/roy.html

Ashton-Warner, S. (1986). *Teacher.* Simon & Schuster: Touchstone.

Bridges to Practice. National Institute for Literacy. http://www.nifl.gov/nifl/ld/bridges/bridges.html

Brookfield, S. (1987). *Developing critical thinkers: Challenging adults to explore alternative ways of thinking and acting.* John Wiley & Sons.

Bruffee, K. (1973). Collaborative learning: Some practical models. *College English, 34,* 579-586.

Bruffee, K. (1986). Social construction, language, and the authority of knowledge: A bibliographical essay. *College English, 48(8),* 773-788.

Bruner, J. (1986). *Actual minds, possible worlds.* Cambridge: Harvard University Press.

Clifford, J. (1981). Composing in stages: The effects of a collaborative pedagogy. *Research in the Teaching of English, 1,* 37-53.

Colvin, R. J. (1997). *I speak English.* 4th edition. Syracuse NY: New Readers Press.

Colvin, R. J. & Root, J. H. (1999). *READ: Reading evaluation—adult diagnosis.* Syracuse NY: New Readers Press.

Connolly, P., & Vilardi, T. (Ed.). (1989). *Writing to learn mathematics and science.* New York: Teachers College Press, Columbia University.

Cooper, C. (1977), Holistic evaluation of writing. In C. Cooper and L. Odell (Eds.), *Evaluating writing: describing, measuring, judging.* Urbana: NCTE.

Diederich, P. (1974). *Measuring growth in English.* Urbana: NCTE.

Emig, J. (1971). *The composing processes of twelfth graders.* Urbana: NCTE.

Enos, T. (Ed.). (1987). *A source book for basic writing teachers*. New York: Random House.

Farrell, T. (1977). Literacy, the basics, and all that jazz. *College Composition and Communication, 38,* 443-449.

Flower, L., & Hayes, J. (1981). A cognitive process theory of writing. *College Composition and Communication, 32,* 365-387.

Foster, D. (1983). *A primer for writing teachers*. Upper Montclair, NJ: Boynton/Cook.

Freire, P. (2000). *Pedagogy of the oppressed*. 30th anniversary edition. New York: Continuum International Publishing Group.

Fromkin, V. & Rodman, R. (1993). *An introduction to language*. 5th edition. New York: Harcourt Brace Jovanovich.

George, D. (1984). Working with peer groups in the composition classroom. *College Composition and Communication, 35,* 320-326.

Gerber, P. & Reiff, H. (1994). *Learning disabilities in adulthood: Persisting problems and evolving issues*. ERIC. http://www.eric.ed.gov (ED 381 675)

Greenbaum, S. (1989). *A college grammar of English*. New York: Longman.

Hartwell, P. (1985). Grammar, grammars, and the teaching of grammar. *College English, 47,* 105-127.

Harwell, J. (2001). *Complete learning disabilities handbook: Ready to use strategies and activities for teaching students with learning disabilities*. 2nd edition. John Wiley & Sons: Jossey-Bass.

Hillocks, G. (1982). The interaction of instruction, teacher comment, and revision in teaching the composition process. *Research in the Teaching of English, 16(3),* 261-78.

Hillocks, G. (1986). *Research on written composition: New directions for teaching*. ERIC. http://www.eric.ed.gov (ED 265 552)

Hoyt, F. (1906). The place of grammar in the elementary curriculum. *Teachers College Record, 7,* 483-84.

Jordan, D. R. (1996). *Teaching adults with learning disabilities*. Melbourne, FL: Krieger

Jordan, D. R. (2000). *Understanding and managing learning disabilities in adults*. Melbourne, FL: Krieger

Kirsch, I. & Jungeblut, A. (1987). *Literacy: Profiles of America's young adults*. Princeton, NJ: NAEP, Educational Testing Service.

Kruidenier, J. (2002). *Research-based principles for adult basic education reading instruction*. National Institute for Literacy.

Kucera, H., & Francis, W. N. (1967). *Computational analysis of present-day American English*. Providence, RI: Brown University Press.

Lavoie, R. (1991). *How difficult can this be? F.A.T. city: A learning disabilities workshop* (DVD). PBS Video.

Learning Disabilities Training and Dissemination Project (2003). *Promising practices: what we learned as pilot programs*. Syracuse NY: ProLiteracy

Lunsford, A. (1978). What we know—and don't know—about remedial writing. *College Composition and Communication, 29,* 47-52.

Lunsford, A. (1979). Cognitive development and the basic writer. *College English, 41,* 38-46.

Macrorie, K. (1984). *Writing to be read* (3rd edition). Rochelle, NJ: Hayden.

McShane, S. (2005). *Applying research in reading instruction for adults: First steps for teachers.* National Center for Family Literacy.

Miller, S. (1983). *Special reading problems.* Syracuse, NY: Literacy Volunteers of America, Inc.

Moffett, J. (1976). *Student-centered language arts and reading.* Boston: Houghton Mifflin.

Murray, D. (1978). Write before writing. *College Composition and Communication, 29,* 375-81.

Myers, M. (1980). *A procedure for writing assessment and holistic scoring.* ERIC. http://www.eric.ed.gov (ED 193 676)

Myers, M. (1985). *The teacher-researcher: How to study writing in the classroom.* ERIC. http://www.eric.ed.gov (ED 261 394)

Northcutt, N. (1975). *The adult performance level study.* Austin, TX: University of Texas.

Payne, N. (2008). *Learning disabilities: Teaching using cognitive mapping strategies.* ProLiteracy Annual Conference, Little Rock, AK.

Perl, S. (1979). The composing processes of unskilled college writers. *Research in the Teaching of English, 13,* 317-336.

Piaget, J. (1954). *The construction of reality in the child.* New York: Basic Books.

Rose, M. (1980). Rigid rules, inflexible plans, and the stifling of language: A cognitivist analysis of writer's block. *College Composition and Communication, 31,* 389-99.

Rose, M. (1984). *Writer's block: The cognitive dimension.* Carbondale: Southern Illinois University Press.

Rosenblatt, L. (1978). *The reader, the text, the poem.* Carbondale: Southern Illinois University Press.

Shaughnessy, M. (1976a). Basic writing. In G. Fate (Ed.) *Teaching composition: 10 biographical essays.* Fort Worth: Texas Christian University Press.

Shaughnessy, M. (1976b). Diving in: An introduction to basic writing. *College Composition and Communication, 27,* 234-30.

Shaughnessy, M. (1977). *Errors and expectations: A guide for the teacher of basic writing.* New York: Oxford University Press.

Smith, C. (2003). *Learning disabilities: The interaction of students and their environment.* 5th edition. Boston, MA: Allyn & Bacon (Pearson Education).

Smith, C. & Strick, L. (1999). *Learning disabilities: A to Z: A parent's complete guide to learning disabilities from preschool to adulthood.* Simon & Schuster: Free Press.

Sommers, N. (1980). Revision strategies of student writers and experienced writers. *College Composition and Communication, 31,* 378-88.

Sonbuchner, G. M. (1991). *Help yourself: Basic learning styles.* Syracuse NY: New Readers Press.

TABE training by Rosemary Matt, National Reporting Systems Liaison for New York State, 1/22/08, BOCES

Van Duzer, C. & Florez, M. C. (1999). *Critical literacy for adult English language learners.* ERIC. htp://www.eric.ed.gov (ED 441 351)

Vogel, S. A. & Reder, S., editors (1998). *Learning disabilities, literacy, and education.* Baltimore, MD: Brookes Publishing Company

Vogel, S. (1993) Teaching suggestions for adults with suspected learning disabilities/ differences. in Colvin, R. J. *Tutor.* 7th edition. Appendix pp. 188-189.

Vygotsky, L. (1962). *Thought and language* (E. Hanfmann & G. Vakar, Trans.). Cambridge: M.I.T.

Wangberg, E., et al. (1984). First steps toward an adult word list. *Journal of Reading.* International Reading Association.

Weaver, C. (1988). *Reading process and practice.* Portsmouth, NH: Heinemann.

Weiner, H. (1986). Collaborative learning in the classroom: A guide to evaluation. *College English, 48,* 52-61.

Wertsch, J., et al. (1980). The adult-child dyad as a problem solving system. *Child development, 51,* 1215-21.

West, F. (1975). *The way of language.* New York: Harcourt Brace Jovanovich.

Wikipedia, a free encyclopedia with millions of articles contributed collaboratively using Wiki software, in dozens of languages. http://www.wikipedia.org

Wilde, S. (1989). Understanding spelling strategies. In K. Goodman and Y. Goodman (Eds.). *The whole language evaluation book.* Portsmouth, NH: Heinemann.

Wilde, S. (1992). *You kan red this!* Portsmouth, NH: Heinemann.

INDEX